Employer Perceptions of the Psychological Contract

David E. Guest

Neil Conway

David Guest is Professor of Organisational Psychology and Human Resource Management at King's College, London. Prior to joining King's, he was Professor of Occupational Psychology and head of the Department of Organisational Psychology at Birkbeck College for 10 years (1990–2000). He has written and researched extensively in the areas of human resource management, employment relations and the psychological contract, motivation and commitment, and careers. He is a member of the editorial advisory board of a number of journals and a Council Member of the Tavistock Institute. His current research is concerned with the relationship between human resource management and performance; the individualisation of employment relations and the role of the psychological contract; flexibility and employment contracts; and the future of the career.

Neil Conway has been a researcher in the Department of Organisational Psychology at Birkbeck College since 1994, where he completed his PhD in Organisational Psychology in 1998. His main research interests include the psychological contract, human resource management, motivation, organisational citizenship behaviours, absenteeism and contingent work. With David Guest, he was the major contributor to the reports on the 1996, 1997 and 1998 *IPD Survey of Employment Relationship*.

The Chartered Institute of Personnel and Development is the leading publisher of books and reports for personnel and training professionals, students, and all those concerned with the effective management and development of people at work. For full details of all our titles, please contact the Publishing Department:

Tel: 020 8263 3387
Fax: 020 8263 3850

E-mail: publish@cipd.co.uk

The catalogue of all CIPD titles can be viewed on the CIPD website:
www.cipd.co.uk/publications

Employer Perceptions of the Psychological Contract

David E. Guest

The Management Centre, King's College, London

Neil Conway

School of Management and Organisational Psychology
Birkbeck College, University of London

First published 2001

Cover design by Curve
Designed and typeset by Beacon GDT
Printed in Great Britain by Short Run Press

British Library Cataloguing in Publication Data
A catalogue record for this book is available from the British Library

ISBN 0 85292 839 4

Chartered Institute of Personnel and Development,
CIPD House, Camp Road, London SW19 4UX

Tel: 020 8971 9000
Fax: 020 8263 3333
Website: www.cipd.co.uk

Incorporated by Royal Charter. Registered charity no. 1079797.

Contents

Foreword

With this report the psychological contract comes of age. It is no longer possible to describe it as simply an academic construct with little or no relationship to what goes on in the workplace. One perhaps surprising finding from this report is that *one in three senior personnel managers say they use the psychological contract to help them manage the employment relationship*. Nine out of 10 agree that it is a useful concept. So it seems that the term is becoming accepted as part of the everyday language of managers, as well as claiming its place as a useful element in the curriculum for students of employee relations.

What is distinctive about this report is that it offers for the first time a picture of the psychological contract as seen by the *employer*. Most previous studies, including those undertaken for the CIPD, have looked at the relationship from the point of view of *employees*. But of course this is only part of the story: every contract needs to have at least two parties. The employer's perspective matters because managers' behaviour is influenced by their beliefs.

The report shows that in some respects – and not those that might have been expected – employers see the relationship rather differently from employees. For example, employers do not believe that on the whole they are meeting employees' expectations on job security. On the other hand we know from earlier research that only a small minority of employees feel insecure. Still more surprisingly, only just over one in four managers say they are meeting their promises to give employees fair treatment, whereas two out of three workers believe they are fairly treated. A majority of managers report that employees are highly motivated to do a good job and that their performance at work has been outstanding. It would be a mistake to dismiss this as springing from feelings of either guilt or a wish to flatter.

This is *not* a picture of employers who believe employees need to be driven in order to deliver high levels of performance.

The report underlines some messages from earlier CIPD research. For example there is little or no evidence that the traditional psychological contract is undergoing radical transformation. Half of the managers believe their organisation has kept its promises about providing opportunities for promotion, and most of the rest say these promises have been met to some extent: *no indication here that organisations are no longer offering 'careers'*. On the other hand managers do not believe that in general they are making unreasonable demands on employees, though evidence from other surveys is that most employees feel they are working very hard and could not be expected to work any harder. The answer to this apparent conflict may lie in the fact that few organisations seek to define in advance what is a reasonable level of effort or application, so that the issue of how far they have kept their promises in this respect is somewhat blurred. The message is still that managers should be looking for their employees to work smarter, not harder.

One finding from this survey is definitely at odds with that from earlier CIPD surveys of employee attitudes. This is that *there was a typically low application of people management practices* in the organisations surveyed. Of the 'core' practices included in the survey, only one in three organisations applied at least half the practices to more than 75 per cent of their workforce. This is a significantly less favourable finding than those from earlier CIPD surveys, though it is in line with those from the 1998 Workplace Employee Relations Survey. The explanation probably lies largely in the more detailed questions in the current survey, which explored not only the number of practices used but how extensively they were applied within individual organisations. It is perhaps somewhat reassuring that employee involvement practices are the most extensively used, since these have been shown to be key to supporting business performance.

A whole new area opened up by this report is the *process by which the psychological contract is established and subsequently renegotiated*. The report distinguishes between three broad kinds of communication between management and workforce. The first is described as job-related and personal communication and includes setting performance targets, performance appraisal and briefings by line management. These methods are generally regarded as very effective, no doubt because they generally allow for feedback from individual employees. A second category of communication occurs mainly around the recruitment process and includes job descriptions, staff handbooks and initial training. Although widely used, these forms of communication are considered to be somewhat less effective. Finally downward communication, for example through company meetings or mission statements, is generally seen as least effective of all.

These findings get away from the idea of the psychological contract as something fixed and immutable that employers are saddled with and cannot escape. They reinforce the need for employers to be aware of the messages they are giving at different stages in the management process and think about how far they are consistent with one another and how they will be understood by employees. The employer is not for this purpose some abstract entity: managers at all levels can have an influence on employees' perceptions of the psychological contract. It is, however, the *relationship between individual employees and their line manager* that is likely to have most influence in framing and managing

employees' expectations. The job of the line manager in motivating employees and harnessing their energies is once more heavily underlined.

So what should managers look out for if they want to manage the psychological contract effectively? One message is about not making promises or commitments that they cannot back up. Management has to see that rhetoric and reality are in line, and that the organisation implements effectively the policies it adopts. The negative findings about public-sector attitudes reflect a failure by managers to deliver in this area. Moreover the awkward truth is that managers can and do influence employee attitudes and expectations, even if they individually have little power to influence delivery.

One final factor underlined by the report is that there is some imbalance in the level of mutual commitment between employer and employees. Although two out of three managers agree that employees are willing to put themselves out for the organisation, only about one half agree that the organisation is willing to put itself out for employees. In other words managers believe there is an unequal bargain and that employees do not benefit from the level of commitment that they themselves are ready to put in. This finding suggests that, if managers want more commitment from employees, they will need to see that the organisation shows more concern about the way in which employees are treated. Arguments about companies' inability to look after their employees in the face of fierce competition in world markets will not get employers off this hook.

Mike Emmott

Adviser, Employee Relations
Chartered Institute of Personnel and Development

Executive summary

◨ This report presents the findings of a survey of 1,306 senior personnel managers – all members of the CIPD – who responded to a questionnaire about the management of the psychological contract. It was originally sent to 3,000 managers, giving a response rate of 43 per cent.

◨ Eighty-four per cent of the managers had heard about the psychological contract, 36 per cent said they used it to help them manage the employment relationship and by the end of the survey 90 per cent agreed that it was a useful concept.

◨ The data were analysed on the basis of a conceptual model that explored the relationship between human resource practices, the promises to employees made and kept by the organisation, the practices used to communicate these promises and a range of outcomes mainly reflecting employee attitudes and behaviour and indicators of the employment relationship.

◨ As in other recent surveys, there was a relatively low application across the workforce of a range of progressive human resource practices. Using a list of 14 core practices, 57 per cent of organisations applied at least half of them to 50 per cent or more of the workforce, and 32 per cent applied at least half to 75 per cent or more of the workforce.

◨ The promises made by the organisation to its employees fell into three main groups, concerned with rewards, information and development, and the context for work. Most promises are made and kept in relation to information and development and fewest are made in relation to the context of work.

◨ Promises are most likely to be kept with respect to not making unreasonable demands on employees and opportunities for promotion. These are two areas where much has been written about the breakdown of the traditional psychological contract. Promises are least likely to be kept with respect to provision of a safe working environment and a range of rewards other than promotion, such as fair pay and job security.

◨ The psychological contract is most likely to be communicated locally through setting of performance targets, performance appraisal and line management briefings. These methods are also considered the most effective. Top-down communication, such as annual meetings with staff and mission statements, are still widely used but are considered to be less effective.

◨ Promises are more likely to be kept where more human resource practices are applied and effective job-related and induction-related communication takes place. Promises are less likely to be kept in large organisations and in the public sector.

◨ Workers are generally seen as co-operative. Sixty-five per cent of managers are satisfied and 15 per cent dissatisfied with the co-operation the organisation receives from its employees.

◨ Employee involvement in key decisions is low. Twenty-four per cent of managers agree and 52 per cent disagree that employees are involved in decisions made by the organisation affecting jobs.

- Employment relations are considered to be good in a majority of organisations. Fifty-nine per cent of managers agree and 20 per cent disagree that the relationship between the organisation and its employees is 'very good'.

- There is a moderate degree of reciprocal commitment. Fifty-two per cent of managers agree and 17 per cent disagree that employees are really committed to working for the organisation. Fifty-five per cent agree and 20 per cent disagree that the organisation is really committed to its employees.

- There are limits to the organisation's commitment to its employees. Sixty-six per cent of managers agree and 12 per cent disagree that employees are willing to put themselves out for the organisation. However, only 53 per cent agree while 22 per cent disagree that the organisation is willing to put itself out for employees.

- Just over half the managers report high employee motivation. Fifty-one per cent agree and 20 per cent disagree that employees are highly motivated to do a good job.

- Levels of innovative behaviour are considered by managers to be too low. Twenty-four per cent agree and 43 per cent disagree that their organisation is satisfied with the amount of innovation and new ideas coming from employees.

- High employee performance is reported in half the organisations. Fifty-one per cent of managers agree and 22 per cent disagree that overall, the performance at work of employees has been outstanding.

- All the outcomes listed above are more positive where managers report that the organisation has kept more of its promises, where there is greater application of human resource practices, where there is effective use of job-related communication and, less important, where the psychological contract is used to help manage the employment relationship.

- Managers report a number of significantly poorer outcomes where there is a recognised trade union at the organisation. There is a tendency for those working in larger organisations also to report poorer outcomes. Outcomes tend to be slightly better in the public sector but this depends partly on whether promises made by the organisation are kept.

- A majority of managers agree that their organisation's management of promises and commitments to employees has a positive impact on a range of employee attitudes and behaviours.

- The findings of this survey support the model of the psychological contract and the case for careful management of the psychological contract reflected in the use of more human resource management, making promises that can be and will be kept and use of job-related communication techniques. It also implies that careful management of the psychological contract makes a positive contribution to effective employment relations.

1 | Introduction

◻ **The traditional model of employment relations based on collective bargaining and joint consultation now no longer applies in most workplaces. Employers therefore need to find a new framework for managing the employment relationship.**

◻ **The psychological contract provides a possible framework for managing contemporary employment relations.**

The employment relationship has been going through a long period of gradual change. During the past two decades the role of trade unions and of collective arrangements has diminished considerably to a point where, as the 1998 Workplace Employee Relations Survey (Cully *et al* 1999) showed, only 36 per cent of workers in establishments employing 25 people or more belong to a trade union, down from 47 per cent in 1990 and 65 per cent in 1980. In the private sector the figures are even starker with only 26 per cent belonging to a trade union. Of course the figures are even lower in smaller establishments where many people now work. In the same way, trade union recognition for purposes of collective bargaining has declined from 64 per cent in 1980 to 53 per cent in 1990 and 42 per cent in 1998. In the private sector, only 25 per cent of establishments employing 25 or more in 1998 recognised a trade union (Millward, Bryson and Forth 2000). In other words, the traditional dominant model of employment relations in which representatives of management and the workforce came together in negotiation and consultation to bargain over and discuss a range of issues no longer operates in most workplaces. Employers therefore need to develop new frameworks for managing the employment relationship.

In looking for an appropriate framework, we might start by recognising the individualisation of the employment relationship. This has a number of features, including the collapse of any role for representative arrangements, except perhaps through work teams, and the emphasis on individual–organisation linkages, manifested, if successful, in high levels of commitment to the organisation. One of the popular mechanisms for achieving such linkages is the use of financial arrangements that tie the individual to the organisation through forms of employee share ownership or profit-sharing. However, these are often restricted to management levels and cannot easily be applied in the public sector.

A separate issue of current interest in employment relations is partnership at work. Spurred on by the TUC and pressure groups such as the Involvement and Participation Association (IPA), the government has endorsed the idea of partnership and provided financial support for partnership initiatives. Despite the strong collaborative emphasis in partnership, the underlying concept of mutuality is likely to make it attractive in unionised workplaces where it might enhance the role of representatives. It is less likely that partnership will be attractive in non-union settings. Yet any framework for considering employment relations must be able to accommodate the majority of workplaces where there is no recognised union presence as well as those where partnership between management and unions might be pursued.

One possible framework for considering the employment relationship across all types of

> **'Support for the importance of the organisation's employment policies and practices in shaping employees' assessment of the state of their psychological contract ... has been found consistently in the CIPD ... annual surveys'**

workplace draws on the idea of the psychological contract. Early definitions viewed the psychological contract as an exchange. For example, Kotter (1973) defined it as 'an implicit exchange between an individual and his organisation which specifies what each expects to give and receive from each other in their relationship'. More recently Herriot and Pemberton (1995) in the UK, placing greater emphasis on the contracting process, defined the psychological contract as 'the perceptions of both parties to the employment relationship, organisation and individual, of the obligations implied in the relationship. Psychological contracting is the process whereby these perceptions are arrived at.' They saw contracting as something that took place primarily between boss and subordinate in the form of a negotiated exchange. The concept of negotiated exchange at the individual level offers distinct parallels with the traditional pluralist exchange of collective bargaining. However, it is inevitably more restricted and will be constrained, among other things, by the wider human resource policy and practice. In other words, the policy context and the ways in which an organisation seeks to communicate and implement its policies will help to shape and perhaps constrain the exchanges out of which the psychological contract between individual and organisation emerges.

Support for the importance of the organisation's employment policies and practices in shaping employees' assessment of the state of their psychological contract and of the employment relationship more generally has been found consistently in the CIPD series of annual surveys among a random sample of the British workforce. These annual surveys confirm the importance of the way in which the psychological contract is managed – or at least the importance of management policy and practice in determining

the state of the psychological contract. To understand the significance of this, we need to reflect on the reasons for the wider interest in the concept of the psychological contract. Rousseau (1995) and others have argued that the traditional psychological contract – reflected partly in the core collective bargaining notion of a fair day's work for a fair day's pay – has broken down, that changes at work have meant that it is increasingly difficult to manage the psychological contract and that this has costs for employees and employers in the form of contract violations and associated disaffection. Although these assertions are contentious, they nevertheless emphasise the importance of finding better ways of managing the psychological contract. First, however, we need a better understanding of how senior managers currently view and believe they manage the psychological contract in their organisations. The survey reported here sought to explore these issues.

The findings presented here are part of a larger study of the employers' side of the psychological contract. In addition to this report, we have conducted a series of detailed case studies. These will be brought together in a later report. Here we concentrate on the findings of a survey of employers. The aims of the survey were:

- to examine whether employers used the psychological contract as a basis for employment policy and if so whether it was considered useful

- to identify the promises and commitments made by employers and their perceptions of whether or not these were kept

- to examine the ways in which the psychological contract was communicated and the relative effectiveness of the various approaches to its communication

◘ to identify the impact of a more or less effective management of the psychological contract for a range of employment relations outcomes

◘ to draw out lessons for policy and practice.

In undertaking this work we used a definition of the psychological contract that we have used in the annual surveys, namely 'the perceptions of both parties to the employment relationship, organisation and individual, of the reciprocal promises and obligations implied in the relationship'. The conceptual framework adopted for the study and the report also has some similarities to that used in our work on employees' perceptions of the state of the psychological contract. It is set out in Figure 1.

The report starts by describing the research process and the characteristics of the sample. In the following chapter the human resource practices that support the employment relationship are outlined. Subsequent chapters look at promises and commitments made and kept, the role of communication, the impact on outcomes of the employment relationship and, finally, the policy implications.

Figure 1 | Theoretical framework

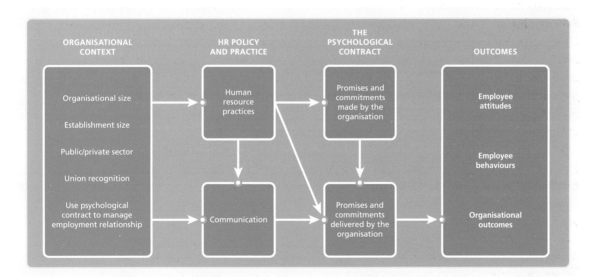

2 | The managers and organisations in the survey

◘ **The survey had an excellent response rate; it was completed by 43 per cent (1,306) of the sample of senior managers.**

◘ **Thirty-six per cent of the senior managers say they already use the concept of the psychological contract to help them manage the employment relationship.**

In June 1999, questionnaires were sent to approximately 3,000 members of the CIPD who, according to CIPD records, were likely to hold senior positions in their organisations. Given an inevitable amount of job change, a number are likely to have been inappropriately directed. Nevertheless, 1,306, or 43.5 per cent, were returned in time for analysis. This is a very good response rate for a survey of this kind among senior managers. We have no clear evidence about the representativeness of those who responded.

Full details of the sample can be found in the appendices. Here we shall briefly say something about the organisations in which they worked and the individuals themselves.

Size of organisation and establishment

Only 1 per cent worked in organisations employing fewer than 10 people, while a further 9 per cent worked in organisations employing between 10 and 50 people. This suggests that we were successful in targeting those who worked in larger organisations. Indeed, 20 per cent worked in organisations employing 100 to 499 employees, 11 per cent in organisations employing 500 to 999, 28 per cent in organisations employing 1,000 to 5,000 employees, and the remaining 31 per cent in organisations employing over 5,000. The establishments were inevitably smaller. Ten per cent worked in establishments employing fewer than 25, 48 per cent worked in establishments employing 25 to 499, and the remainder were in large establishments with 500 or more, including

20 per cent in establishments with more than 1,000 employees. We are therefore dealing with predominantly medium and large-sized organisations and establishments.

Sector

Forty-three per cent of the sample worked in the private services sector, 20 per cent in manufacturing, 3 per cent in utilities and the remaining 34 per cent in the public sector.

Trade union recognition

Not surprisingly, given the size of the organisations and establishments, 61 per cent recognised trade unions. There is a significant correlation between size and recognition. Recognition is also significantly higher in the public sector than in the private sector; the comparative figures are 92 per cent for the public sector and 45 per cent for the private sector. Where trade unions are recognised, membership is fairly evenly spread. In 20 per cent of organisations, membership is estimated at less than 25 per cent; in a further 29 per cent of organisations, membership is at between 25 and 50 per cent; in 34 per cent of organisations it is estimated to be between 51 and 75 per cent; and finally in 17 per cent of organisations it is estimated to be over 75 per cent of the workforce. Union recognition and union density is therefore a potentially important influence on the nature of the deal in a majority of organisations in this sample.

Individual roles

As expected, the vast majority of respondents – 86 per cent – work in some aspect of personnel, human resource or training management. The remainder fill a variety of roles.

Job level

Twenty-two per cent in the sample operate at director level, 40 per cent are in a senior executive or group role, 33 per cent are managers, and the remaining 5 per cent describe themselves as senior officers. This confirms that we were quite successful in targeting those in senior and policy-making roles.

Tenure

The average organisational tenure of respondents was 9.1 years.

Are their views representative?

We asked the managers whether they felt their views on the issues addressed were likely to represent those of the organisation. In other words, are they in some sense an agent or representative of the employer? Nine per cent were very confident that they spoke for the organisation and a further 59 per cent felt that to 'a very great extent' their views represented those of the organisation. Twenty-eight per cent felt that they 'somewhat' represented the organisation while only 4 per cent felt their views represented the organisation 'a little' or 'not at all'.

Familiarity with the concept of the psychological contract

Over a number of years the term 'the psychological contract' has increasingly been used in personnel management circles. Yet it may not have struck a chord with policy makers and practitioners. To check this we explored levels of awareness and use of the concept. Prior to the survey, 84 per cent had heard of the concept. By the end of the survey, 90 per cent agreed that it is a useful concept. Thirty-six per cent were sufficiently familiar with it and valued it to the extent that they used it to help them manage the employment relationship. This confirms the view that it is a concept that has utility. One of the issues we can explore is whether its use has any impact on a set of practices and outcomes that might be associated with effective management of the psychological contract.

We have now set out the characteristics of the organisations and the individuals who replied to the questionnaire. While there is no reason to believe that many of these characteristics will have a major bearing on policy and practice, we shall include them as background and control variables in our analysis as indicated in the conceptual framework. As already noted, use of the psychological contract to help in the management of employment policy may be something of an exception. If it is effective, then it should help to explain some of the variation in policy and practice.

3 | Human resource practices

☒ **The responses confirm the findings of other management surveys in showing a relatively low use of 'high commitment' human resource practices across industry.**

☒ **Three 'bundles' of practices were identified covering employee contribution and involvement, employment relations practices and personnel techniques.**

☒ **The most extensively used practices are those designed to ensure employee contribution and involvement.**

In the annual CIPD surveys of workers' perceptions of the state of the employment relationship, we have asked employees about their experience of human resource practices. Analysis of their responses has consistently shown that those who experience more of what are sometimes termed 'high commitment' practices also report that their psychological contract is in a better state in the sense that more promises are delivered by management and they feel more fairly treated and trust management more. This in turn is associated with higher satisfaction and other positive attitudinal and behavioural outcomes. We have therefore included a similar list of human resource practices in the management survey in the expectation that managers might report a similar set of associations. If this proves to be the case, it would offer further support for the view that the policy context and the way in which it is played out in the form of specific human resource practices has an important role in determining perceptions of the state of the psychological contract and related employment relations outcomes.

One of the challenges when asking managers about human resource practices is to determine how widely they are applied. Responses to a question such as 'Do you use appraisals?' could be answered with a yes when it applies to 5 per cent or 95 per cent of the workforce. One of the assumptions underpinning a high commitment model is that a form of single status will be in place and that practices should apply to all or at least most workers (allowing variation for those who are subcontracted or temporary workers). To capture this, we asked about the proportion of the workforce to which each practice applied. We used 14 items covering core human resource practices, but went a little beyond those normally associated with 'high commitment' to include an item on the use of consultation as a means of involvement. The results are shown in Table 1.

Table 1 is divided into three sections. This is because we undertook a factor analysis to determine whether the practices clustered together in any meaningful way. In the literature on human resource management, there has been some discussion of 'bundles' of practices. Through this analysis we detected three potential bundles:

1 concerned with processes to achieve commitment and involvement

2 concerned with what might be termed employment relations issues

'Part of the argument about the impact of human resource management is that there needs to be a wide range of practices in place for it to have its full effect.'

3 concerned with certain technical aspects of personnel work (this bundle does not hang together very well). In the context of the debate on the psychological contract, they are the sort of practices and techniques that might benefit from the use of an organisational psychologist.

The results in Table 1 show some considerable variation in the use of practices. The processes to achieve involvement are used by a majority of organisations for a majority of employees. Employment relations practices either apply to very few or to almost all employees. The use of personnel techniques is more varied and less consistent. There is a surprisingly low use of

Table 1 | Use of human resource practices

Practices	% of workforce to which the practice applies					
	none	1–25%	26–50%	51–75%	76–99%	all
Processes to achieve involvement						
Tries to make the jobs of employees as interesting as possible	4	13	24	27	19	13
Actively uses teamworking where possible	3	12	18	23	23	21
Keeps employees informed about business issues	1	8	14	20	24	32
Provides opportunities for training or development	0	9	17	23	28	22
Tries to get employees involved in workplace decision-making	5	25	27	17	14	10
Carries out equal opportunity practices in the workplace	3	8	12	16	22	38
Provides regular employee performance appraisals	4	7	11	13	19	47
Employment relations practices						
Has a works council or consultative process to involve employees	31	6	7	6	11	39
Has a stated policy of deliberately avoiding compulsory redundancies	46	4	4	5	8	33
Has provisions to help employees deal with non-work responsibilities	16	21	13	9	12	29
Personnel techniques						
Uses psychometric tests as a standard part of the selection process	28	41	14	7	7	3
Tries to fill vacancies from inside the organisation	4	17	30	22	21	6
Has conducted a company-wide staff attitude survey	40	3	3	3	6	45
Relates some part of pay to individual performance	18	22	12	10	12	25

Note: Numbers are rounded and will therefore not always sum to 100 per cent.

psychometric tests for all employees and a split on performance-related pay with approximately 40 per cent either making a lot or very little use of it.

Part of the argument about the impact of human resource management is that there needs to be a wide range of practices in place for it to have its full effect. We are therefore interested in knowing not just which practices are more or less popular, but how many are applied to a significant proportion of the workforce in each organisation. We can conduct a count of how many practices are applied to more than 50 per cent of the workforce, which would suggest that they affect a majority of the workforce, and how many are applied to more than 75 per cent, which suggests something approaching the kind of total coverage that some advocates of human resource management would welcome. The results are shown in Figures 2 and 3.

The results show that in 12 (0.9 per cent) organisations there are no practices that apply to more than 50 per cent of the workforce, while in 47 (3.6 per cent) organisations there are no practices that apply to more than 75 per cent of the workforce. At the other extreme, there are only seven (0.5 per cent) organisations that apply all the practices to more than 50 per cent of the workforce, and only one (0.1 per cent) that applies them all to more than 75 per cent. Put another way, 57 per cent of the organisations apply at least half of the practices to more than 50 per cent of their workforce, and 32 per cent apply at least half to more than 75 per cent of the workforce.

Given the size of these organisations, this represents a relatively low level of adoption of human resource practices. Indeed, it confirms the findings of the 1998 Workplace Employee Relations Survey (Cully *et al* 1999) and the Future

Figure 2 | Count of HR practices, where each practice applies to more than 50 per cent of the workforce

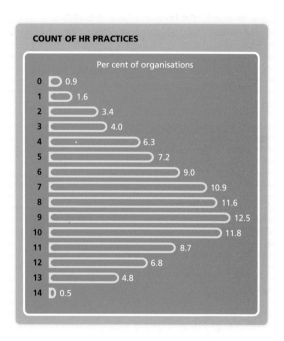

COUNT OF HR PRACTICES

Per cent of organisations

0	0.9
1	1.6
2	3.4
3	4.0
4	6.3
5	7.2
6	9.0
7	10.9
8	11.6
9	12.5
10	11.8
11	8.7
12	6.8
13	4.8
14	0.5

Figure 3 | Count of HR practices, where each practice applies to more than 75 per cent of the workforce

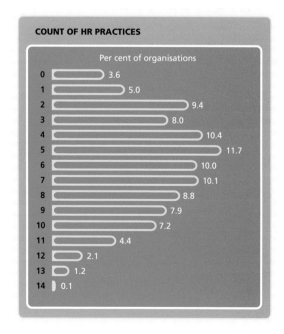

COUNT OF HR PRACTICES

Per cent of organisations

0	3.6
1	5.0
2	9.4
3	8.0
4	10.4
5	11.7
6	10.0
7	10.1
8	8.8
9	7.9
10	7.2
11	4.4
12	2.1
13	1.2
14	0.1

> **' ... there is considerable variation across the organisations in both the number of human resource practices used and in the proportion of employees covered by specific practices.'**

of Work Survey (Guest *et al* 2000). Both surveys – based on establishments and organisations that on average were somewhat smaller in size than those represented in the present survey – reported low levels of adoption of human resource management.

We can explore whether the background factors described in the previous chapter help to explain any of the variation in the adoption of practices. Taken together, they explain 9 per cent of the variation in responses. (In the regression analysis, the beta weights for the significant items were: use of the psychological contract in employment policy 0.25, p<.001, establishment size 0.13, p<.001 and a recognised union 0.06, p<.05.) More human resource practices are in place in those organisations that use the psychological contract as a policy device and in larger establishments. The presence of a recognised trade union also has a small but significant positive association with the number of practices in place. It is likely that issues such as business strategy, human resource strategy and a range of related issues that are beyond the scope of this survey also play an important part in helping to explain the use and the coverage of human resource practices.

Summary

In summary, we have found a typically low application of human resource practices across a majority of the workforce in the organisations surveyed. The most extensively used practices are those designed to gain employee involvement and contribution. Background factors included in the survey help to explain some of the variation in use of human resource practices, the most important being the use of the psychological contract to help shape the employment relationship. The results confirm that there is considerable variation across the organisations in both the number of human resource practices used and in the proportion of employees covered by specific practices. This provides us with a good opportunity to explore whether the greater use of practices is associated with a more developed psychological contract and with outcomes of benefit to the organisation or its employees.

4 | The content of the psychological contract

☑ **Organisations are most likely to make promises and to believe they keep them in the area of information provision, involvement and development. They are more cautious about making and claiming to keep promises about rewards.**

☑ **There is a strong link between the use of more human resource practices and both the number of promises made and kept.**

☑ **Managers in the public sector say that their organisations make fewer promises and keep fewer of those that they do make.**

Introduction

In this chapter, we explore managers' accounts of the promises and commitments made by organisations and the extent to which they have been met. The core of the psychological contract concerns the exchange of promises and commitments and, as already noted, most studies focus on employees' perceptions of whether management has kept its promises or violated them in some way. In this case, we are exploring somewhat similar issues but from the organisation's perspective. It is worth bearing in mind that the exchange that lies at the heart of the psychological contract also incorporates promises and commitments made by workers. Although any detailed exploration of these is beyond the scope of this study, some of the commitments managers might seek from workers, such as motivation for work and a readiness to offer suggestions for improvements, are included in the list of outcomes presented in Chapter 6.

The choice of promises and commitments is inevitably somewhat arbitrary. We collected a set of items based on a review of the literature. We also provided space for managers to extend the list if we omitted anything they considered to be important in their organisation. In the event, 9 per cent offered additional items. For each of the 13 items on the list, we first asked whether a promise

had been made and second whether it had been kept. Since we are dealing with what is inevitably an area of uncertainty, we asked whether there was no promise, a suggestion of a promise, a strong suggestion of a promise or a clear and formal commitment, possibly written down.

The promises and commitments made by organisations

The results are shown in Table 2. They are divided into three groups that emerged as coherent groupings from a statistical analysis. This gives us some clues to policy priorities and focus. The first group of items is concerned with promises about a range of rewards, both intrinsic and extrinsic, including pay, promotion, recognition and interesting work. The second group is concerned with information and development and includes training as well as aspects of communication. The final group covers the context for work, including a pleasant working environment, job security and fair treatment. The only 'rogue' item is a safe working environment, which should fall in the third group but statistically fits slightly better in the second group.

We noted that 9 per cent of the managers had added items to the list. The most frequently cited additional items fell into two main groups. The first was concerned with a range of equal

> ' ... employers are cautious in making promises about rewards,
> somewhat more enthusiastic about the context for work and
> most enthusiastic about information and development.'

opportunity and family-friendly issues such as freedom from harassment, no discrimination, nursery provision and an opportunity to work from home. The second dealt with the promise of an open consultative style of management with an emphasis on involvement and a union role. Other more idiosyncratic items included health and recreation facilities and the promise that work would be fun!

It can be seen from Table 2 that employers are cautious in making promises about rewards, somewhat more enthusiastic about the context for

work and most enthusiastic about information and development. This fits fairly closely with the evidence about the human resource practices that managers reported to be in place. They were most likely to report the presence of practices concerned with development and involvement. There is a marked reluctance to make promises about interesting work and about workload. If we were to summarise the psychological contract from an employer's perspective, they appear to offer employees a safe working environment in which they will be fairly treated, well-informed – particularly about their own performance – and

Table 2 | Promises and commitment made by organisations

	No promise made	Suggestion of a promise; nothing actually said or written	Strong suggestion of a promise; nothing actually said or written	Written or oral promises have been made
Rewards				
An attractive benefits package	24	20	27	29
Interesting work	27	29	33	11
A fair rate of pay	13	16	35	36
Opportunities for promotion	18	24	33	25
Recognition for innovative or new ideas	25	27	20	27
Information and development				
Training and development opportunities	2	6	19	73
Feedback on performance	4	11	24	61
Open two-way communication	6	15	35	43
A safe working environment	3	5	21	71
The context for work				
Reasonable job security	29	19	32	19
Not to make unreasonable demands on employees	39	25	24	12
A pleasant working environment	23	26	33	18
Fair treatment	5	10	28	56

Note: Numbers are rounded and will therefore not always sum to 100 per cent.

provided with opportunities for training and development. While it is quite likely that the organisation will suggest or imply promises about extrinsic rewards, it will be reluctant to promise job security or interesting work and, despite some emphasis on fair treatment, employees would be unwise to expect that the employer will not make unreasonable demands on them from time to time.

Of course this crude pen picture of what employers offer hides a lot of variety. We can gauge this by looking at the number of written or oral promises made by organisations and the number of items on which no promises are made. This reveals that 28 per cent of the organisations make seven or more written or oral promises – what can be considered to be definite promises – on over half the items listed. In contrast, 6 per cent make no promises on seven or more of the items. The average number of items on which written or oral promises are made, according to the respondents, is 4.76, while the average number on which no promise is made is 2.17.

There is therefore considerable variation in the promises made and it is important to link this to a range of outcomes. There are two prior steps. The first is to identify the kinds of organisation that are likely to make more or less promises. An analysis of the background factors that help to explain this reveals that the number of human resource practices in place, which in themselves often imply a promise, shows a much stronger association with the number of promises made than any other factor. (In this and in subsequent analyses, we based the count on the number of practices that were applied to more than 50 per cent of the workforce.) Use of the psychological contract in employment policy and the size of the organisation are also associated with the number of promises, while fewer are reported by managers working in the public sector. The actual results for a composite set of promises made are shown in Figure 4. The next step is to explore not just whether promises are made but whether they are kept.

Figure 4 | Factors associated with the number of organisational promises made

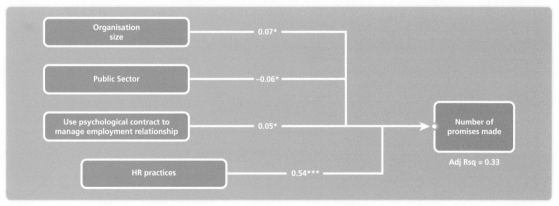

Notes

1 * significant (p<.05); ** strongly significant (p<.01); *** very strongly significant (p<.001). Only significant associations are displayed.

2 The adjusted R-square (Adj Rsq) indicates the per cent (when multiplied by 100) of variance explained in the outcome by the 'predictor' variables. In the present case, for example, the background variables explain 33 per cent of the variation in the number of promises made.

Do organisations keep their promises?

The questionnaire asked managers in those organisations that had either made a strong suggestion of a promise or provided an actual written or oral promise whether the promise had been kept. Possible responses ranged from 'not met' through 'met to some extent' to fully 'met' and even 'exceeded'. The results are shown in Table 3. We again undertook a factor analysis to determine whether the items clustered together in a distinctive way. This provided us with a somewhat different set of combinations. However, they make some sense. The first is concerned with the context of work and is similar to the category of promises with the same name. However, it now includes a safe working environment and excludes job security. Job security appears instead in the second group concerned with rewards. The third group is concerned with information, involvement and development and includes familiar items on training and development, on feedback and communication, but now also the items on recognition and interesting work.

Table 3 | Are promises kept?

% (n ranges between 572 and 1,187)	exceeded	met	met to some extent	not met
The context of work				
A safe working environment	0	17	67	16
Not to make unreasonable demands on employees	12	44	40	4
A pleasant working environment	4	33	47	16
Fair treatment	1	27	64	8
Rewards				
An attractive benefits package	3	27	54	15
A fair rate of pay	2	27	58	13
Reasonable job security	5	24	56	15
Opportunities for promotion	3	50	43	4
Information, involvement and development				
Training and development opportunities	2	46	45	6
Feedback on performance	2	41	51	5
Open two-way communication	6	48	37	8
Recognition for innovative or new ideas	9	46	38	6
Interesting work	3	47	43	6

Note: Numbers are rounded and will therefore not always sum to 100 per cent.

The predominant response of managers is a cautious one. Typically, promises and commitments have been 'met to some extent'. They are more certain that they have met promises in the area where most organisations are likely to have made them in the first place, namely information, involvement and development. This extends just as strongly to recognition and interesting work, about which rather fewer promises were made. Some aspects of the reward package and the working environment are the areas where promises are least likely to have been kept. Promises are rarely likely to be exceeded; the only hint of an exception comes with respect to not making unreasonable demands on employees where some organisations presumably believe they have leant over backwards to be fair.

What emerges is a picture of organisations where the management representatives believe they have largely kept their promises. One of the more interesting comparisons is with the responses of employees. We do not have directly comparable data for all the items, but one of the areas where employees are most likely to feel that promises are not kept over the years has been workload. This may be an area in which there is a risk that organisational representatives have a somewhat false picture. In the 1999 employee survey, promises were most likely to be rated as kept in the area of job security followed by a career and fair pay with interesting work low down the list. However, we are not necessarily comparing like with like so we can do no more than signal possible areas where perceptions of whether promises have been kept are not always shared by employer and employee.

In what contexts are promises kept?

Do those organisations that use the psychological contract as a policy device or that have a lot of human resource practices in place believe they keep their promises to a greater extent? The evidence from the employee surveys of their psychological contract suggests that this might well be the case. In this context we can test it through a regression analysis. The results are shown in Figure 5.

Figure 5 | Factors associated with keeping promises

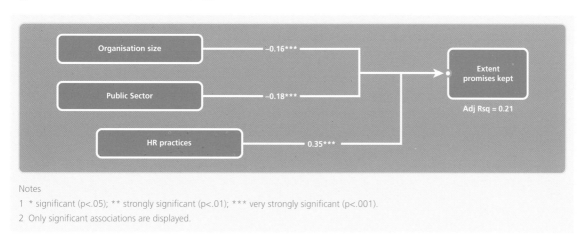

Notes

1 * significant (p<.05); ** strongly significant (p<.01); *** very strongly significant (p<.001).

2 Only significant associations are displayed.

' ... senior managers are cautious about claiming that their organisations keep promises in full, particularly if they work in larger organisations and in the public sector.'

The results confirm the importance of adopting a larger number of human resource practices. Altogether, the various background factors help to explain 21 per cent of the variation in responses. As well as looking at the overall number of human resource practices, we examined the importance of the three clusters or 'bundles' that we identified. This revealed that greater use of involvement-related processes and personnel techniques are both associated with keeping promises. In contrast, greater use of employee relations-related practices is not associated with keeping promises. This raises some interesting issues about the existence of a more pluralist, possibly lower trust context where employment relations receives a higher emphasis and where more rigorous criteria are imposed to determine whether promises and commitments are kept. More specifically the presence of a trade union helps to make management more aware of promises that have not been kept. In the event, a union presence has no significant impact on the extent to which promises are kept. On the other hand, it is not altogether surprising to find that promises are less likely to be kept in larger organisations and also in the public sector compared with the private sector. The public sector findings fit with the 2000 survey of employees (Guest and Conway 2000), which showed that employees in the civil service reported a significantly poorer psychological contract – measured in terms of promises kept, fairness and trust – than those in the private sector as well as in health and local government. In other words, we may detect a public sector factor but we need to be a little cautious in generalising too far within the public sector. Finally, it is notable that the use of the psychological contract in employment policy is not significantly associated with the extent to which promises are kept.

Summary

In summary, we have now reviewed the extent to which promises are made and kept. We have found that senior managers are more likely to believe that their organisations make and keep promises in the area of employee information, involvement and development. However, separate evidence suggests that they may be a little optimistic concerning how far they keep promises about providing interesting work and recognition and more particularly avoiding making unreasonable demands on employees. Nevertheless, by and large senior managers are cautious about claiming that their organisations keep promises in full, particularly if they work in larger organisations and in the public sector. They are more confident that they keep them where they have more human resource practices in place.

5 | Communicating the psychological contract

◩ **The widespread use of job-related techniques to communicate the psychological contract confirms the importance of the boss–subordinate relationship at the heart of the psychological contract.**

◩ **Corporate communication activities such as mission statements and reports to all staff are rated as less effective in ensuring a positive psychological contract than job-related communication.**

Introduction

One of the key challenges for any organisation that seeks to manage the psychological contract is how to communicate it effectively to employees. This can occur at a variety of levels and at various points within an employment cycle with an organisation. If the potential means of communicating a psychological contract are not used, then the organisation leaves employees to make their own assumptions, with the resultant risk of faulty expectations. At the same time, excessive or unconvincing rhetoric from management can, as we hinted in the previous chapter, lead to unmet expectations. In this chapter we therefore look more closely at what senior managers say about the way in which their organisations seek to communicate the psychological contract. Since we have already ascertained that only about a third use the psychological contract as a policy device, we might expect some considerable variation and also might find that those who are using it to shape employment policy show a rather different pattern of communication.

Methods of communicating the psychological contract

We defined 'communication' very widely and included 13 possible forms of communication.

Once again we undertook the statistical process of factor analysis to determine whether communication methods clustered together in any meaningful way. We found three clear factors, which are presented in Table 4. The table shows, in the left-hand column, the percentage of organisations where managers say the organisation uses this method to communicate its promises and commitments. This ranges from 100 per cent of organisations with respect to the recruitment process, to 82 per cent with respect to other briefing groups. We need to be a little cautious in accepting these figures as indicators of methods used to communicate the psychological contract, bearing in mind that most organisations do not use the psychological contract as a policy device. However, this in itself need not preclude the use of these various forms of communication to say something about what the organisation offers its workers and expects in return. At the very least, the responses point to the wide range of communication devices in use in contemporary organisations. The rest of Table 4 shows managers' judgements about whether the mode of communicating the psychological contract is effective on a five-point scale, ranging from 'not at all effective' to 'very effective'. Ratings of effectiveness were provided only by those who reported that their organisation used the particular form of communication in connection with the psychological contract.

The factor analysis, as noted above, produced three distinct factors. The first is concerned with what we have termed job-related and personal communication. With the exception of team targets, this is extensively used and generally considered to be at least 'somewhat' effective and often rather more than 'somewhat' effective. The second set of items is concerned with initial and bureaucratic communication. It covers what happens to newcomers in terms of recruitment and induction and what is often formalised either in a job description or in a staff manual or handbook. These forms of communication are again widely used but considered to be slightly less effective than job-related and personal communication; there are particular doubts about the value of job descriptions as a means of communication. Finally, corporate downward communication is rather less widely used to communicate promises and commitments and when it is used it is generally seen as the least effective approach. Mission statements, which can

Table 4 | Methods of communication

	used	not at all effective	slightly effective	somewhat effective	effective	very effective
Job and personal communication						
Individual objectives and targets	97	3	11	34	35	17
Team targets	84	6	21	35	28	10
Performance appraisal	96	2	11	33	38	15
Informal day-to-day interaction	99	2	11	32	36	18
Briefing by line management	98	2	12	35	37	13
Training and development	99	1	10	36	36	17
Initial and bureaucratic communication						
Recruitment processes	100	1	9	33	44	13
Job descriptions	92	14	23	35	22	6
Induction and initial training	99	2	10	32	39	16
Staff handbook/manual	88	6	13	29	35	17
Corporate downward communication						
Annual company meetings with, and reports to, staff	84	11	23	26	25	15
Mission statements	91	15	29	27	19	11
Other briefing groups	82	5	16	37	32	10

Note: Numbers are rounded and will therefore not always sum to 100 per cent.

' [The results suggest] that it is helpful to embed the
communication practices associated with the psychological
contract within a wider human resource framework.'

be a particular source of overenthusiastic rhetoric,
are especially likely to be perceived as no more
than moderately effective.

Although it appears from these results that a wide
range of approaches to communication helps to
set and reinforce the psychological contract, in the
judgement of senior managers it is those closest to
day-to-day performance and to the job that are
most effective. This supports a view that the boss–
subordinate relationship lies at the heart of the
psychological contract.

We explored the background factors associated
with both the range of communication practices
used and their rated effectiveness. When we look
at the overall use, then only two background
factors show a significant association; indeed,
background factors explain only 8 per cent of the
variance in responses. The first factor is the use of
a greater range of human resource practices. In

one sense this is a slightly spurious association
since the list of human resource practices includes
aspects of communication. The other background
factor that showed a significant association is size
of organisation; again, it is no surprise to find that
larger organisations use more forms of
communication.

We can also examine the link between
background factors and managers' rated
effectiveness of the combined set of
communication practices in use. In this case,
background factors explain 34 per cent of the
variation. As Figure 6 indicates, use of a greater
range of human resource practices is by far the
most important influence. This suggests that it is
helpful to embed the communication practices
associated with the psychological contract within a
wider human resource framework. Use of the
psychological contract in employment policy shows
a modest positive association with effectiveness of

Figure 6 | Factors associated with overall communication effectiveness

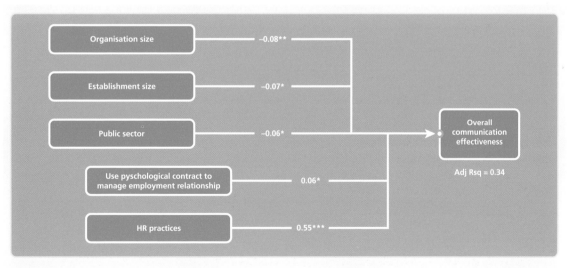

Notes

1 * significant (p<.05); ** strongly significant (p<.01); *** very strongly significant (p<.001).

2 Only significant associations are displayed.

communication. There are small but significant negative associations with size of organisation and establishment and with working in the public sector. This again confirms that public sector organisations may be perceived as less successful in ensuring the effective delivery of policies and practices, including those associated with communication of the psychological contract.

The results are similar if we explore each of the three sets of practices independently. Use of human resource practices is positively associated with each. Although the public sector is rated less effective at job-related and top-down communication, it is now rated better than the private sector at communication associated with initial induction and provision of bureaucratic information. Larger organisations are significantly less effective except with respect to top-down communication. There are some small variations in

background factors associated with each set of communication practices, but on the whole the differences are minor.

Is effectiveness of communication associated with delivery of the psychological contract?

There are various ways of assessing the effectiveness of different communication techniques and indeed of the management of the psychological contract as a whole; we turn to this in the next chapter. However, we might expect to find an association between rated effectiveness of communication and the judgement of whether or not promises have been kept, ie whether or not the psychological contract has been delivered. We explore this by analysing the association between background factors, including effectiveness of communication practices and the delivery of promises. The results are shown in Figure 7.

Figure 7 | Factors associated with extent organisations keep promises when communication is included

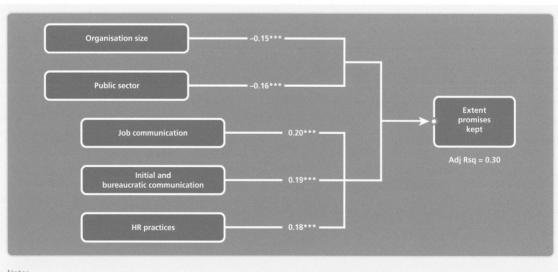

Notes

1 * significant (p<.05); ** strongly significant (p<.01); *** very strongly significant (p<.001).

2 Only significant associations are displayed.

We separated the three main types of communication to determine whether they had a different effect. The results show that this was indeed the case. The effectiveness of two sets of communication activities – those associated with job performance and with initial introduction to the role – have a strong association with keeping promises. Top-down, corporate communication does not have the same apparent influence, even where it is effective. Use of more human resource practices retains the positive association with keeping promises that we identified in Chapter 4. Similarly, the size of organisation and working in the public sector continue to show a negative association with the extent to which promises are kept.

Summary

In summary, we have shown that organisations use a wide range of communication devices and that even where they do not make explicit use of the psychological contract in employment policy, managers are ready to associate these means of communication with their, perhaps implicit, management of the psychological contract. The communication devices fall into three groups and while these are associated with similar background factors, there is some initial indication in this chapter that they are not all equally effective in achieving their purpose and that even when they are effective they have a different impact on delivery of promises associated with the psychological contract. In the next chapter we shall be able to look further at the link between each set of communication practices and a range of outcomes associated with the employment contract.

6 | Outcomes from the psychological contract – the state of the employment relationship

☒ **Managers who say their organisation keeps its promises to its employees also report consistently more positive employee attitudes and behaviour.**

☒ **Organisations that apply more human resource practices to a majority of the workforce report more positive employee attitudes and behaviour.**

☒ **Job-related communication more than induction-based or top-down communication is associated with positive outcomes.**

☒ **Managers suggest that employees are more likely to put themselves out for the organisation than the organisation is for its employees.**

☒ **Managers rate most outcomes positively, but are dissatisfied with the amount of innovative ideas coming from employees and low levels of employee involvement.**

Introduction

In this final chapter of results, we are interested in whether the management of the psychological contract is considered to be effective. To do this, we obtained assessments from managers on a range of issues associated with the state of the employment relationship. Many of these have been covered in previous surveys that have focused on the employees' perspective. There were 26 items in this section. An initial factor analysis revealed two major and three minor factors. The two major factors that emerged covered the contribution that employees make to the organisation and the things the organisation does for employees. These are of interest in their own right, but they cover so many items that we subdivided them on *a priori* grounds and identified a total of nine sets of items, including the three minor factors. We report the findings for these below.

Many of the items included in the large factor covering the contribution that employees make to the organisation can be seen as part of the employees' input to the psychological contract. It is unlikely that many or indeed any of the items will take the form of explicit promises, but they reflect what many managers might consider to be some of the 'obligations' of employees within a balanced exchange. At the very least they represent a set of aspirations of the outcomes or return on investment in the psychological contract. The assumption embedded in this chapter is that the initiative in developing the psychological contract lies with management. If the organisation makes, communicates and keeps certain promises to its employees, then in return it might expect a range of positive responses reflected in the employees' contribution to the employment relationship.

> ' If the organisation makes, communicates and keeps certain promises to its employees, then in return it might expect a range of positive responses ... .'

The employees' contribution to the organisation

In this section we cover a wide range of issues, such as trust, co-operation, motivation, citizenship behaviour and performance. Trust is perhaps best considered as a rather separate dimension. Unless there is an acceptable level of trust, as perceived by managers and employees, then there is unlikely to be a willing contribution on many other issues. In other analyses we have therefore treated trust, alongside fairness and the delivery of promises, as a core dimension reflecting the state of the psychological contract rather than an outcome from it. In this context, the items are concerned with management trust in employees. We therefore start with trust before moving on to analyse other outcomes.

Trust in employees

The two items concerned with trust explore how far the organisation can place trust in its employees. The results are shown in Table 5.

The two items work reasonably well as a short scale, with an alpha reliability score of .63. (The alpha reliability provides an indication of how well the two items hang together as a scale and can

therefore be combined to form a single composite measure of trust. Normally we would look for an alpha score above .70, though a score above .60, as in this case, is sometimes acceptable. The alpha scores on all the short scales used in this chapter are shown in Appendix 3 and, unless otherwise stated, are all above .65.) There is relatively little variation in responses on this item, with a strong cluster around the 'agree' category. Only a small proportion, averaging 10 per cent across the two items, suggest that employees cannot be trusted. On the other hand, there is little evidence of a really enthusiastic endorsement of trust in employees. If anything, employees offer a wider range of responses when confronted with a similar question. Typically, about a third say they trust management 'a lot' while around 20 per cent trust management 'only a little' or 'not at all'.

We looked at the background factors that explain what variation there is in responses. The background and policy factors explain 18 per cent of the variation, a rather lower proportion than on many other items. The main influences are shown in Figure 8.

The key influence on whether employees can be trusted is whether management has kept its promises and commitments to employees – whether it has kept its side of the psychological

Table 5 | Trust in employees

	strongly disagree	disagree	uncertain	agree	strongly agree
The organisation can trust employees to keep their promises and commitments	1	6	17	68	8
Employees can be trusted to look after the interests of the organisation	1	12	21	58	8

contract. This reinforces the exchange component of the psychological contract implying that if management keeps its promises and commitments, then employees in turn can be trusted to do the same. In addition, a larger number of human resource practices and effective job-related communication also contribute. Deliberate use of the psychological contract is associated with higher trust while the presence of a recognised trade union is associated with lower management trust in employees.

Co-operation from employees

The two items in Table 6 present an assessment of levels of co-operation by employees.

Figure 8 | Factors associated with organisational trust in employees

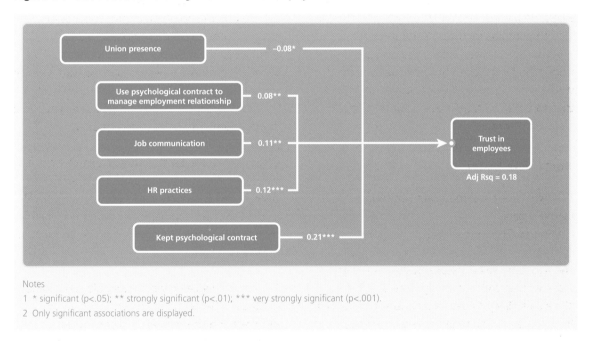

Notes
1 * significant (p<.05); ** strongly significant (p<.01); *** very strongly significant (p<.001).
2 Only significant associations are displayed.

Table 6 | Co-operative behaviour by employees

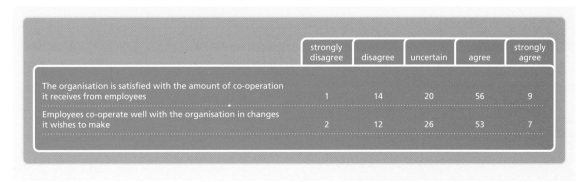

	strongly disagree	disagree	uncertain	agree	strongly agree
The organisation is satisfied with the amount of co-operation it receives from employees	1	14	20	56	9
Employees co-operate well with the organisation in changes it wishes to make	2	12	26	53	7

There is a fairly high degree of uncertainty about the level of co-operation and few extreme responses on these items. On balance, a little over 60 per cent of managers are positive about the level of co-operation from employees, while about 15 per cent are dissatisfied. The result of the regression analysis that attempts to explain these differences is shown in Figure 9.

The various background and policy items explain 20 per cent of the variation in responses. They confirm again the view among managers that when the organisation keeps its promises, then the employee response is more positive. In addition, greater use of human resource practices and effective job-related communication are positively linked to assessments of co-operation. So too is the deliberate use of the psychological contract to manage employment relations. In contrast, the presence of a recognised trade union is strongly

associated with lower levels of co-operation. This confirms management perceptions that have emerged in a number of earlier sections, suggesting that a union presence is seen as unhelpful to a positive psychological contract and associated outcomes.

Employee involvement

A reasonable level of co-operation is normally a prerequisite for employee involvement in decision-making. The two items in Table 7 cover aspects of employee involvement. They focus on involvement in decisions at the organisational rather than the job level. Responses on this issue are much less positive, although the reasons for this may reflect either management reluctance to encourage involvement at this level or employee reluctance to become involved. The items address involvement in general issues and in job-related issues. With

Figure 9 | Factors associated with co-operative behaviour by employees

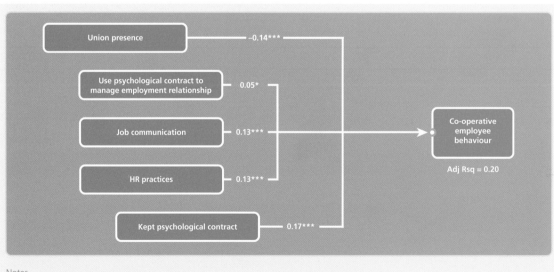

Notes
1 * significant (p<.05); ** strongly significant (p<.01); *** very strongly significant (p<.001).
2 Only significant associations are displayed.

Table 7 | Employee involvement

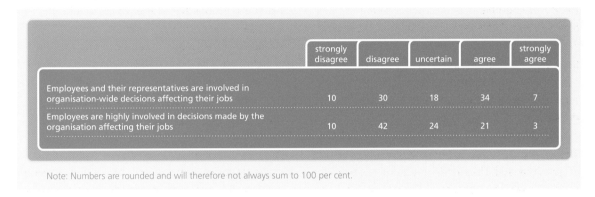

	strongly disagree	disagree	uncertain	agree	strongly agree
Employees and their representatives are involved in organisation-wide decisions affecting their jobs	10	30	18	34	7
Employees are highly involved in decisions made by the organisation affecting their jobs	10	42	24	21	3

Note: Numbers are rounded and will therefore not always sum to 100 per cent.

Figure 10 | Factors associated with employee involvement

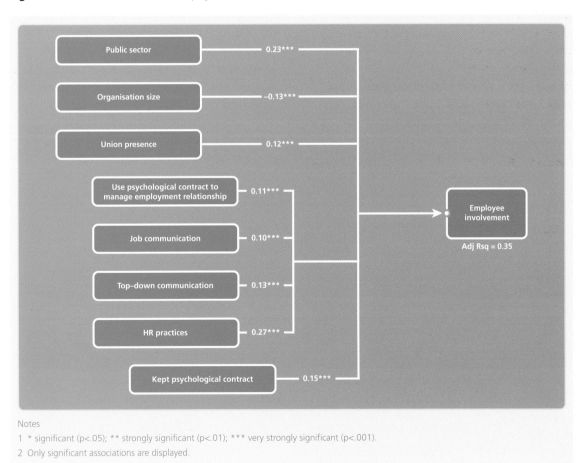

Notes
1 * significant (p<.05); ** strongly significant (p<.01); *** very strongly significant (p<.001).
2 Only significant associations are displayed.

respect to the general issues, there is an almost equal division between those who say employees and their representatives are and are not involved in decisions. When it comes to decisions affecting jobs, which could occur at a variety of levels and in which employees might legitimately claim to have a stake, employee involvement is much lower; indeed, over half the managers say employees are not involved.

We might expect that a number of background factors help to explain these differences in levels of employee involvement. As Figure 10 indicates, background factors included in the analysis explain 35 per cent of the variation in responses.

The first point to note in Figure 10 is that quite a large number of background factors have some sort of independent association with employee involvement. Those showing the strongest associations are the use of more human resource practices – which we might expect since some of these practices reflect attempts to involve employees – and the public sector, where there is a long tradition of involvement through formal institutions and of a degree of professional autonomy at the job level. Other positive

associations are with two of the three communication dimensions, including job-related communication, a belief that management has kept its promises and the presence of a recognised trade union. This may reflect the level at which the content of involvement is pitched and the reference to employees and their representatives; or it may be a consequence of the pressures exercised by a union presence. The use of the psychological contract to manage the employment relationship is associated with more involvement, while organisation size is associated with less.

Employee relations

Co-operation and involvement are closely associated with employee relations. Two items covered perceptions of the overall state of the employment relationship. They are shown in Table 8.

Almost 60 per cent agree that relations between management and employees are good, while 20 per cent disagree. In response to one of the standard questions about employment relations, less than half agree that employees and management are on the same side. Despite quite a

Table 8 | Employee relations

	strongly disagree	disagree	uncertain	agree	strongly agree
Overall, the relationship between the organisation and its employees is very good	2	18	21	52	7
Employees and management are on the same side in this organisation	5	21	29	39	7

Note: Numbers are rounded and will therefore not always sum to 100 per cent.

' ... there is some indication that managers, like many workers, still see some basis for "us and them" attitudes and behaviour.'

high level of uncertainty in the responses on this item, there is some indication that managers, like many workers, still see some basis for 'us and them' attitudes and behaviour. We might expect this to be stronger where a trade union is present. We can explore whether this is indeed the case by examining the background factors associated with a more positive or negative assessment of the employment relationship. The responses are shown in Figure 11.

The background factors explain 35 per cent of the variation in responses. However, contrary to expectations, the presence of a recognised trade union has no association with the assessment of the state of employee relations. Instead, the key

factor, in the view of managers, is whether or not the organisation has kept its promises. This is very similar to the responses we obtain when asking a somewhat similar question of employees and it confirms that the onus for good employment relations lies very much with management. Once again, use of more human resource practices, deliberate use of the psychological contract to manage the employment relationship and more effective use of job-related and top-down communication are also associated with good employment relations. These results therefore provide further evidence of the importance of the psychological contract and the policies and practices that reinforce it in establishing a positive employment relationship.

Figure 11 | Factors associated with employee relations

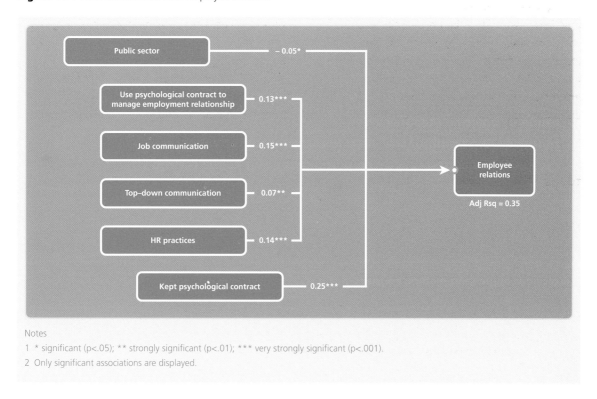

Notes

1 * significant (p<.05); ** strongly significant (p<.01); *** very strongly significant (p<.001).

2 Only significant associations are displayed.

Employee commitment

There are again two items covering employee commitment to the organisation. They are shown in Table 9.

Once again there is a familiar pattern of results, with about half providing a positive response and approximately 20 per cent indicating that commitment among employees is relatively low.

Table 9 | Employee commitment

	strongly disagree	disagree	uncertain	agree	strongly agree
Employees are really committed to working for this organisation	2	15	31	45	7
Employees identify with the values of this organisation	4	18	30	41	8

Note: Numbers are rounded and will therefore not always sum to 100 per cent.

Figure 12 | Factors associated with employee commitment

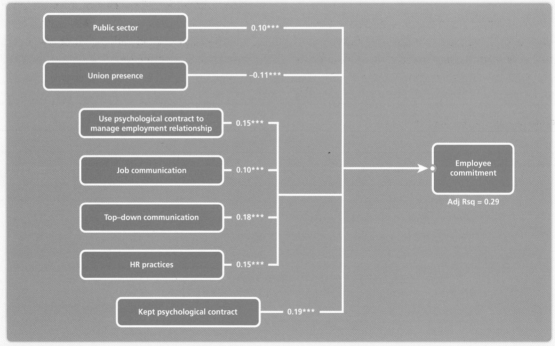

Notes
1 * significant (p<.05); ** strongly significant (p<.01); *** very strongly significant (p<.001).
2 Only significant associations are displayed.

Figure 12 shows the results when we trace the background and policy influences on variations in employee commitment. Together these items explain 29 per cent of the variation in responses. Four items have the largest influence and again confirm the importance of a targeted management of the psychological contract. The four are:

◻ the extent to which promises are kept

◻ the effectiveness of corporate, top-down communication

◻ the number of human resource practices in place

◻ the use of the psychological contract to manage the employment relationship.

A union presence has a negative association and working in the public sector has a positive association with the level of commitment. Effective communication of issues concerned with job performance is also positively associated with commitment. However, the concept of organisational commitment implies a different level of communication and attachment, and the results and greater weight given to corporate communication confirm this.

Employee motivation

Employee motivation was covered with the two items shown in Table 10.

On this topic we can again see few extreme responses, but also some variation in assessments of employee motivation with around a quarter saying their employees are not highly motivated. In seeking to explain variations, we again used a regression analysis incorporating all the background measures and practices. Together these accounted for 26 per cent of the variation in responses. The results in Figure 13 show the specific items associated with higher or lower motivation among employees.

Table 10 | Employee motivation

	strongly disagree	disagree	uncertain	agree	strongly agree
Employees here are highly motivated	4	24	28	39	4
Employees here are highly motivated to do a good job	1	19	29	45	6

Note: Numbers are rounded and will therefore not always sum to 100 per cent.

The results in Figure 13 reveal what is an increasingly familiar pattern. Key items associated with higher motivation are:

◻ keeping management promises associated with the psychological contract

◻ communicating effectively on job-related issues

◻ greater use of human resource practices.

Public sector managers report that their employees are more motivated, but a trade union presence is associated with lower motivation.

Employee citizenship behaviour

Citizenship behaviour is a term used to describe activities that extend beyond the standard requirements set out in a job description. They imply an element of voluntary behaviour on the part of the employee and we might expect them to occur more often in contexts where employees believe that they are well treated and have a positive psychological contract. The two items in Table 11 were used to measure citizenship behaviour.

Figure 13 | Factors associated with employee motivation

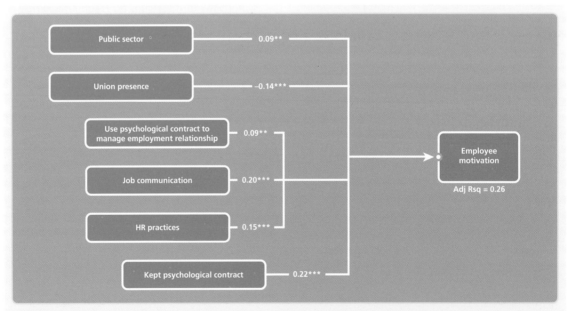

Notes
1 * significant (p<.05); ** strongly significant (p<.01); *** very strongly significant (p<.001).
2 Only significant associations are displayed.

> 'Citizenship behaviour is associated with more effective job-related communication, management keeping its promises and greater use of human resource practices.'

The responses in Table 11 are quite positive, with a large majority of managers agreeing that employees take on additional responsibilities and put themselves out for the organisation. At the same time, there are variations in response and the factors affecting this are highlighted in Figure 14.

The analysis shows that the background and policy factors explain 15 per cent of the variation in responses. The familiar pattern of associations is apparent again. Citizenship behaviour is associated with more effective job-related communication, management keeping its promises and greater use

Table 11 | Employee citizenship behaviour

	strongly disagree	disagree	uncertain	agree	strongly agree
Employees are willing to take on responsibilities beyond their job descriptions	2	9	15	59	15
Employees are willing to put themselves out for the organisation	1	11	22	57	9

Figure 14 | Factors associated with employees' citizenship behaviour towards the organisation

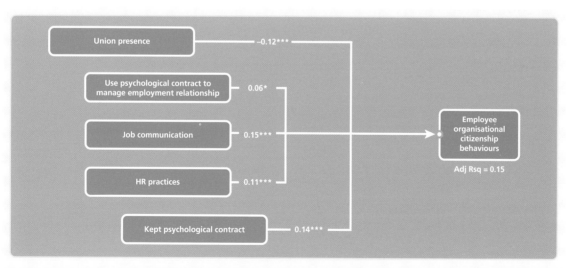

Notes

1 * significant (p<.05); ** strongly significant (p<.01); *** very strongly significant (p<.001).

2 Only significant associations are displayed.

Table 12 | Employee innovation

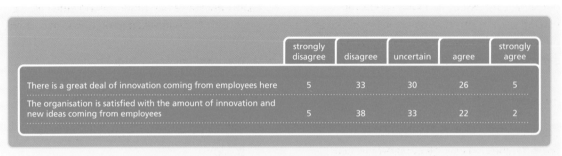

	strongly disagree	disagree	uncertain	agree	strongly agree
There is a great deal of innovation coming from employees here	5	33	30	26	5
The organisation is satisfied with the amount of innovation and new ideas coming from employees	5	38	33	22	2

Note: Numbers are rounded and will therefore not always sum to 100 per cent.

Figure 15 | Factors associated with employee innovation

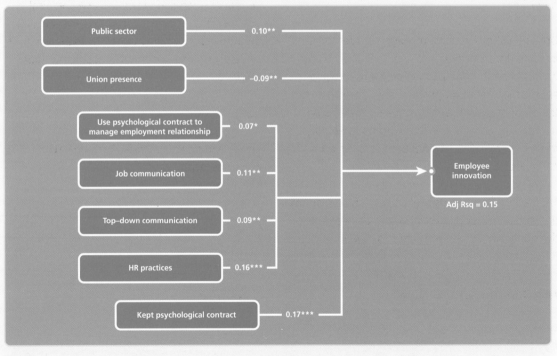

Public sector — 0.10**

Union presence — –0.09**

Use psychological contract to manage employment relationship — 0.07*

Job communication — 0.11**

Top–down communication — 0.09**

HR practices — 0.16***

Kept psychological contract — 0.17***

Employee innovation

Adj Rsq = 0.15

Notes
1 * significant (p<.05); ** strongly significant (p<.01); *** very strongly significant (p<.001).
2 Only significant associations are displayed.

of human resource practices. There is also a weak but significant association with use of the psychological contract in employment policy and a rather stronger negative association with the presence of a recognised trade union.

Innovative behaviour

One variation on citizenship behaviour might be the willingness to engage in innovative activity. Given the dynamic nature of contemporary organisations, this is a characteristic that organisations may be keen to foster. It was again measured with two items, which are shown in Table 12.

Unlike most other items, management responses indicate dissatisfaction with the level of employee contribution through innovation. Only 24 per cent are satisfied, while 43 per cent are dissatisfied with the amount of innovation from employees, a point reinforced by the 38 per cent who disagree that there is a great deal of innovation coming from employees.

The background factors explain only 15 per cent of the variation in employee innovation and some of the significant associations are quite weak.

Nevertheless, the familiar pattern emerges once again. Innovative behaviour among employees is more likely to be reported in organisations where:

◻ management keeps its promises

◻ there is effective job-related communication

◻ there are more human resource practices in place.

Innovation is also more likely in the public rather than the private sector, in organisations where there is effective top-down corporate communication and where the psychological contract is used to manage employment policy. Innovative behaviour is judged by management to be less likely where there is a recognised trade union.

Employee performance

The two items shown in Table 13 deal with employee performance.

Table 13 | Employee performance

	strongly disagree	disagree	uncertain	agree	strongly agree
Overall, the performance at work of employees has been outstanding	2	20	27	45	6
The organisation is extremely satisfied with the performance of its employees	2	19	24	47	7

Note: Numbers are rounded and will therefore not always sum to 100 per cent.

Both items show a generally positive evaluation of performance, although a little over 20 per cent are unwilling to endorse the use of the highly positive words to describe their employees' performance.

An analysis of the background and policy items included in the survey that help to distinguish those who are more or less positive about employee performance indicates that they help to explain 19 per cent of the variation in responses. The specific pattern is summarised in Figure 16.

Figure 16 repeats the very familiar pattern of three factors strongly associated with superior employee performance.

1 the effectiveness of communication on job-related issues

2 whether management promises that make up the psychological contract have been kept

3 the number of human resource practices in place.

Once again the use of the psychological contract to manage the employment relationship has a small positive association. Managers working in the public sector provide higher ratings of performance, but where there is a recognised trade union, managers' ratings of employee

Figure 16 | Factors associated with employee performance

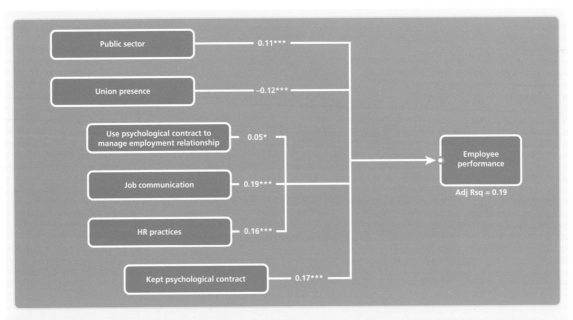

Notes
1 * significant (p<.05); ** strongly significant (p<.01); *** very strongly significant (p<.001).
2 Only significant associations are displayed.

' ... the results show that a careful and targeted management of the psychological contract appears to pay dividends.'

performance are lower. While we might expect communication linked to job performance to have a positive association with ratings of performance, further confirming that such communication is effective, it is interesting that the other types of communication are not associated with employee performance, even when they are considered to be effective.

Employee performance is undoubtedly one of the key outcomes from an organisational perspective and the results show that a careful and targeted management of the psychological contract appears to pay dividends.

Employee turnover

The final aspect of the employee contribution is reflected in a measure of employee turnover and retention. We are assuming here that management would prefer to retain key

employees and the items are phrased to assess whether the desired level of labour turnover and retention is being achieved. The results are shown in Table 14.

Over a third of the managers report that labour turnover is higher than they would like and just under a quarter believe their organisation is unsuccessful in retaining key employees. On the other hand, well over half are satisfied with their current turnover and retention.

To explain the variations in turnover and retention, we undertook the usual regression analysis. The two items, when combined, have an alpha reliability score of .59. This is rather lower than all the other pairs but provides some justification for combining them for the regression analysis. The results of the regression analysis are presented in Figure 17.

Table 14 | Employee turnover

	strongly disagree	disagree	uncertain	agree	strongly agree
The level of labour turnover in the organisation is higher than the organisation would like	17	40	8	24	11
This organisation is successful in retaining high quality employees	4	19	18	50	10

Note: Numbers are rounded and will therefore not always sum to 100 per cent.

The background and policy factors explain 19 per cent of the variation in responses. In Figure 17 a negative association indicates that the variable is associated with lower labour turnover and we can see that all the items except organisation size are negatively associated with labour turnover. Once again, the key factors associated with the desirable outcome of retaining sufficient key employees are:

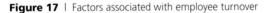 management keeping its promises to employees

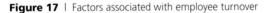 greater use of human resource practices.

This is the only outcome with which the effective use of job-related techniques to communicate the psychological contract shows no significant association. The presence of a recognised trade union is also strongly associated with a more satisfactory level of staff retention. A similar finding has been reported in a number of other studies. The use of the psychological contract in employment policy again has a small but positive association with better staff retention.

Conclusions

We have now covered 10 outcomes that reflect employee contribution either in terms of positive attitudes or behaviour. On most items, management assessments are broadly positive; at the same time they are rather cautious, with few extreme responses, indicating either uncertainty about the outcomes or a reluctance to generalise across the workforce as a whole. A consistent pattern of associations between these outcomes and various background, policy and practice factors has emerged. In almost all cases, the outcome is rated as more positive where managers judge that the organisation has kept its promises

Figure 17 | Factors associated with employee turnover

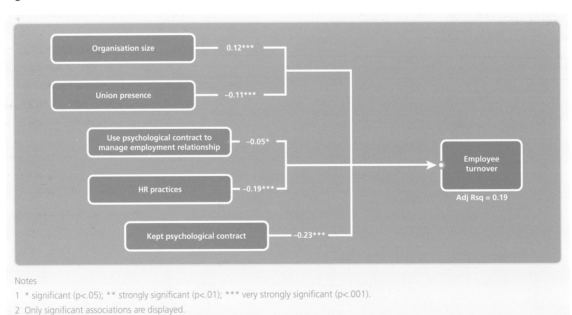

Notes

1 * significant (p<.05); ** strongly significant (p<.01); *** very strongly significant (p<.001).

2 Only significant associations are displayed.

to employees, has adopted a larger number of the 'high commitment' human resource practices and has been effective in communicating job-related information relevant to the psychological contract. The use of the psychological contract to manage employment relations also has a small but consistently positive association with outcomes. Effective use of top-down corporate communication has an inconsistent but generally positive link to a number of outcomes, but the third category of communication devices – what we termed initial induction and bureaucratic communication – has no link to outcomes. We should perhaps not be surprised about this since it is directed largely at newcomers to the organisation and may have an important role in shaping early perceptions of the psychological contract rather than in affecting outcomes.

In addition to items concerned with assessment of the employee contribution, a smaller number addressed the outcomes directed towards employees; in other words, they assessed management perceptions of the contribution the organisation makes to its employees. These are covered in the next section.

The organisation's contribution to its employees

The organisation's commitment to employees

Two items turned conventional commitment questions around to explore how far the organisation was committed to its employees. The descriptive results are shown in Table 15.

The results show some reluctance among managers to accept that the organisation is committed to its employees. Indeed, only slightly over half the managers were prepared to endorse the two statements and the responses to the second statement are distributed in an almost identical manner to those for employee commitment to the organisation in the similarly worded item in Table 9. The failure of senior personnel managers to provide a strong endorsement of their organisation's commitment to its employees raises all sorts of intriguing questions.

Table 15 | The organisation's commitment towards employees

	strongly disagree	disagree	uncertain	agree	strongly agree
The organisation feels a great deal of loyalty towards its employees	4	18	21	44	13
This organisation is really committed towards its employees	4	16	26	48	7

Note: Numbers are rounded and will therefore not always sum to 100 per cent.

Figure 18 | Factors associated with the organisation's commitment towards employees

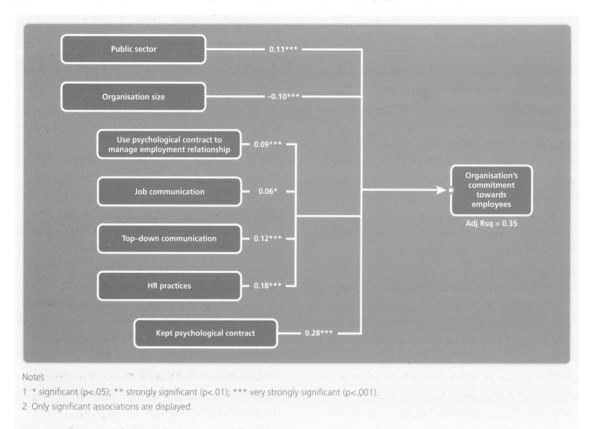

Notes
1 * significant (p<.05); ** strongly significant (p<.01); *** very strongly significant (p<.001).
2 Only significant associations are displayed.

' ... organisations that keep their promises to employees also show greater commitment to employees. So too do those that apply a greater range of "high commitment" human resource practices.'

The results of the analysis exploring background and other factors that explain variations in levels of organisational commitment to employees are shown in Figure 18. The various factors explain an impressive 35 per cent of the variation in responses and once again they conform to the familiar pattern. Perhaps not surprisingly, organisations that keep their promises to employees also show greater commitment to employees. So too do those that apply a greater range of 'high commitment' human resource practices. Other factors associated with greater commitment to employees are:

☐ effective use of top-down communication

☐ use of the psychological contract to manage the employment relationship

☐ being in the public sector.

Effective use of job-related communication has a small positive association with organisational commitment to employees. Greater organisation size is associated with lower commitment to employees. More generally, these results once again confirm the exchange element in the psychological contract in that the factors that are associated with greater organisational commitment to employees are also those that are judged by managers to result in greater employee commitment to the organisation.

Organisational citizenship towards employees

Two items explored how far the organisation is prepared to engage in a form of 'citizenship behaviour' towards employees. In so far as the concept parallels that applied to employees, it implies that the organisation may go beyond its minimum obligations to them (see Table 16).

Although the pattern of responses is broadly positive, it falls far short of a ringing endorsement of a willingness by organisations to make an effort to help employees. Indeed, if we compare these responses with those on parallel items in Table 11, we can see that this sample of senior managers is acknowledging that employees are more willing to put themselves out to help the organisation than the organisation is to help employees. This implies a degree of asymmetry in the exchange at the heart of the psychological contract.

Table 16 | Organisation's citizenship behaviour towards employees

	strongly disagree	disagree	uncertain	agree	strongly agree
The organisation is willing to put itself out to help its employees	4	18	25	44	9
Organisation is willing to extend itself to help employees	2	13	22	54	8

Note: Numbers are rounded and will therefore not always sum to 100 per cent.

Figure 19 shows the factors that explain variations in perceptions of the organisations' 'citizenship' towards their employees. The various items included explain 36 per cent of the variation in responses. Once again we can see that those organisations that keep their promises to employees and adopt more human resource practices are also more likely to put themselves out for their employees. Indeed, both of these background factors could be construed as indicators of just that propensity. More effective communication at both job and corporate level and use of the psychological contract to frame employment policy also have a positive association, while organisational size is associated with lower levels of organisational citizenship.

Fairness of the exchange

There is one final pair of items that summarises managers' perceptions of the fairness of the exchange between the organisation and its employees. The responses are shown in Table 17.

We can see from the responses that a majority of managers believe the deal is fair. There are 18 per cent who disagree. We can get some idea of the reasons for this by looking at the second item. Responses reveal that 16 per cent believe that the organisation invests more in employees than it gets in return. Ideally, we would have asked a further question to explore whether managers believed that employees put in more than they got

Figure 19 | Factors associated with organisations' citizenship behaviour towards its employees

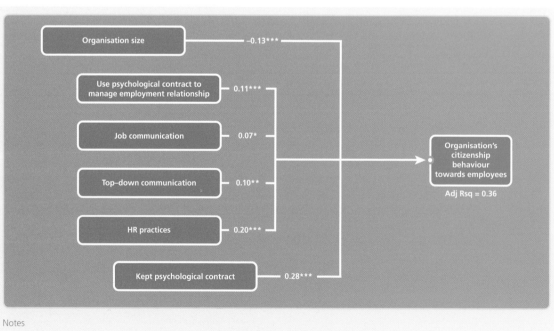

Notes

1 * significant (p<.05); ** strongly significant (p<.01); *** very strongly significant (p<.001).

2 Only significant associations are displayed.

in return. The responses to items in the two previous subsections suggest that a number may well believe that this is the case. Leaving this aside, both items presented here indicate that a little over 60 per cent of managers believe that the exchange – the deal – is fair.

Unlike all the other pairs of items, these two did not meet the requirements to be combined as a single scale. In exploring the background influences on fairness, we therefore focus on the first of the two items, since it is the more general assessment of fairness. The background and other factors associated with fairness are shown in Figure 20.

Table 17 | The fairness of the exchange

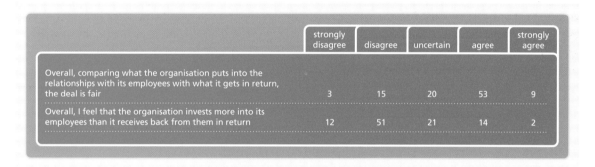

	strongly disagree	disagree	uncertain	agree	strongly agree
Overall, comparing what the organisation puts into the relationships with its employees with what it gets in return, the deal is fair	3	15	20	53	9
Overall, I feel that the organisation invests more into its employees than it receives back from them in return	12	51	21	14	2

Figure 20 | Factors associated with exchange fairness

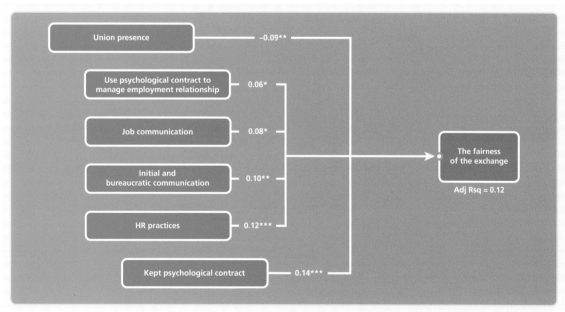

Notes

1 * significant (p<.05); ** strongly significant (p<.01); *** very strongly significant (p<.001).

2 Only significant associations are displayed.

> **'The presence of a recognised trade union is associated with management perceptions of a less fair exchange.'**

The background factors explain a relatively modest 12 per cent of the variation in responses. As so often, keeping promises in the psychological contract and the number of human resource practices show a highly significant association. So too do job-related and induction-related communication practices and, marginally, use of the psychological contract in employment policy. The presence of a recognised trade union is associated with management perceptions of a less fair exchange. Although we shall not show the detailed results for the second item, the pattern of associations is very similar, except that top-down communication replaces induction-related communication.

Overall assessment of the impact of the management of the psychological contract

A final set of six items sought a more general assessment of the impact of the way in which the organisations' management of their promises and commitments to employees influenced a range of core outcomes. The results are shown in Table 18.

Although there may be some value in considering each of these impacts separately, a factor analysis reveals that they emerge strongly as a single factor providing an overall evaluation of the impact of the management of the psychological contract (as a combined scale, these items have an alpha reliability score of .91). Indeed, a glance at Table 18 reveals that the ratings across the various outcomes are very similar and broadly positive.

Despite this, and in line with the earlier analysis, there is some indication that the balance of advantage lies with the organisation. The most positive benefits are identified in the areas of employee performance and commitment, closely followed by employment relations, all of which offer distinct benefits for the organisation. Benefits for employees, reflected in well-being and trust, are considered to be rather lower.

Using this overall measure as an indicator of managers' general assessment of the impact of the psychological contract, we can examine the background factors that explain variations in their overall assessment. The results are summarised in Figure 21 and show that background and other factors explain 40 per cent of the variation. Keeping promises, all three sets of communication devices, use of more human resource practices and use of the psychological contract in policy have a positive association.

Summary

We have now presented all of the 'outcomes' from the management of the psychological contract. They reveal a relatively consistent pattern of associations between aspects of policy and practice and the various outcomes. In Chapter 7 we address some of the implications of these results.

Table 18 | Impact of management of the psychological contract

	definite negative impact	slight negative impact	no effect	slight positive impact	definite positive impact
Impact of organisation's management of its promises and commitments on:					
Employee performance	3	8	17	51	21
Employee commitment	4	11	19	48	19
Employment relations	3	11	19	48	18
Employee well-being	3	10	36	41	9
Employee motivation	4	15	23	48	10
Employee trust in the organisation	8	17	24	39	12

Note: Numbers are rounded and will therefore not always sum to 100 per cent.

Figure 21 | Impact of the management of the psychological contract

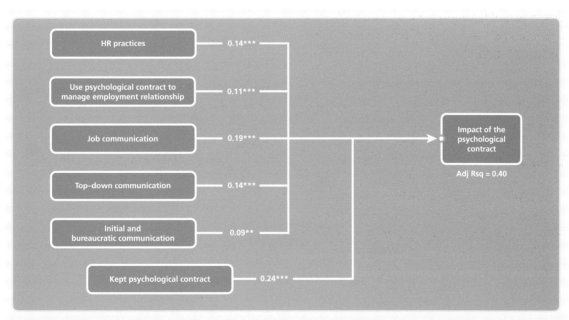

Notes

1 * significant (p<.05); ** strongly significant (p<.01); *** very strongly significant (p<.001).

2 Only significant associations are displayed.

7 | Conclusions and policy implications

◻ **The findings suggest that rather contrary to expectations, the traditional psychological contract – based on promises of promotion and fair pay – is alive and well.**

◻ **Using the psychological contract to help manage the employment relationship has a small but consistent association with positive outcomes.**

◻ **Two simple recommendations to managers emerge from the results of the survey: first, introduce more 'high commitment' human resource practices; second, don't make promises you can't keep.**

In this final chapter, we draw together the findings and assess their implications for the use of the psychological contract as a framework for managing employment relations. In doing so, it is worth bearing in mind again that this survey is part of a larger study of the management of the psychological contract and it will be important to reinforce or possibly challenge some of the findings from the survey with detailed accounts of how the process of managing the psychological contract is played out in practice.

The survey is based on the responses of just over 1,300 senior members of the CIPD. This point is emphasised here to indicate that we are not dealing with a general sample of managers or even of personnel managers. We might reasonably expect this group of senior professionals to be somewhat more sophisticated in their approach to policy than a random sample of people in personnel positions throughout the UK. Because they are senior, these managers might also be expected to have an important role in the formulation and execution of employment relations policy. At the same time, they may be slightly less aware than some middle level managers of how policy is played out on the ground and therefore of the outcomes on which

they were asked to comment. Indeed, there was some indication in the responses that the more senior the manager, the more positive their responses, although we should perhaps not read too much into this.

The use of the psychological contract in policy analysis

One of the first important substantive findings from the survey is that as many as 36 per cent claimed that they already used the concept of the psychological contract to help them manage the employment relationship. Prior to the survey, 84 per cent said that they had heard of the concept, but by the end of the survey 90 per cent agreed that it was a useful concept. This confirms the argument presented in the opening chapter that the psychological contract has potential as a framework within which to consider the contemporary employment relationship. Even those who do not currently use it could relate to the notions of reciprocal promises and commitments and an exchange between the organisation and workers that operates at a number of different levels. Indeed, it could be argued that some managers took almost too readily to the concept, as reflected in the

> ' ... the psychological contract is represented in the promises and commitments, and the *state* of the psychological contract is reflected in the extent to which promises have been delivered.'

impressive endorsement of techniques used to communicate the psychological contract even by those who do not currently use it in the formulation of employment relations policy and practice.

At the outset, we presented a simple model within which to explore the management of the psychological contract. It is no coincidence that it draws on and has strong parallels with the more fully developed model used in recent years in the annual CIPD surveys to explore workers' perceptions of the state of the psychological contract. The model accepts the importance of the wider organisational setting, including its size, sector and union representation. It emphasises the importance of adopting and applying widely a range of human resource practices as a reflection of broad employment relations policy and practice. The model views the mechanisms to communicate the psychological contract, which are likely to operate at a variety of levels in the organisation and to complement and indeed partly overlap with human resource practices, as important additional elements shaping both the number of promises made and the extent to which promises are kept – or at least perceived to have been kept. All of these factors are then expected to have an impact on the outcomes of the psychological contract. In other words, the psychological contract is represented in the promises and commitments, and the *state* of the psychological contract is reflected in the extent to which promises have been delivered. Since we have viewed the psychological contract as an exchange, it is plausible to assume that where more of the promises that have been made are kept, employees will respond by showing more positive attitudes and behaviour. By implication, the initiative for a positive psychological contract lies with management, the policies they operate and

the promises they make and keep. When promises are made and kept, particularly when they are reinforced by a range of human resource practices and effective communication of the promises, then workers will respond.

The key findings

So what have we found? First we have found, in line with other recent surveys, that organisations are reluctant to apply many human resource practices to the whole or even a sizeable majority of the workforce. An exception to this, at least as reported in this survey, is that a wide range of communication devices are used and one of their purposes, implicitly or explicitly, is to communicate features of the psychological contract – or what the organisation offers its workers and perhaps expects in return. Based on statistical analysis, we found that our list of 13 communication devices divided into three clusters. The first cluster – a set of job-related activities such as communicating individual and team targets, performance appraisal and briefing by line management – was widely used and widely judged to be effective. Second, a set of more formal activities associated with induction and familiarisation with a new job, such as use of recruitment processes and a job description, was also very widely used but not considered to be quite as effective. Finally, a number of more corporate, top-down devices – such as annual meetings of staff and mission statements – were quite widely used and seen to be only moderately effective in communicating the psychological contract.

Organisations seem most prepared to make promises and commitments to employees about provision of information and about development. This includes feedback on performance and training and development. They are markedly more reluctant to make promises on issues that we know from other sources concern many workers, such as the demands made on their time. They are much more divided about promising a range of rewards. A quarter promise nothing for innovative or new ideas and a quarter make no promises about interesting work. On the other hand, it was somewhat surprising to find that almost 60 per cent still make promises about opportunities for promotion. There is a strong overlap between the human resource practices in place and the nature of the promises made. Indeed the presence of a specific human resource practice often implies a promise. It appears that the practices and the promises about which organisations are most enthusiastic are primarily concerned with engaging and involving workers in task performance.

As well as applying practices and making promises related to the development of capacity for and involvement in job performance, managers also believe this is the area in which they are most likely to keep their promises. Those who have made promises about rewards are rather less sure about keeping these promises. The same applies to promises about the working context and in particular, somewhat surprisingly, promises about providing a safe working environment. Sixteen per cent say they have made promises but failed to keep them with respect to both a safe and a pleasant working environment. This may reflect the greater focus and priority apparently given to job performance.

We noted at the outset that one of the reasons for the growing interest in the psychological contract was the popular assumption that the traditional psychological contract had broken down and that promises about a secure job and a career for life based on steady promotion could no longer be made or kept. Furthermore, organisational change

and competitive pressures imposed ever greater demands on workers and their time. It is therefore very interesting to note that many managers in this sample do not seem to accept these assumptions. Fifty-eight per cent say their organisations are still making, or at least strongly implying, promises about promotion and only 4 per cent say that such promises are not being kept, the lowest for any item. In addition, although far fewer – only 36 per cent – say they promise not to make unreasonable demands on workers, among those who do make this promise, again only 4 per cent say such promises are not kept and 12 per cent say they even exceed their promise. These findings suggest that, contrary to some claims, the traditional psychological contract is still alive and well in a large number of organisations.

The value of the model of the psychological contract

The model that informs the study works well. In particular, when we look at the outcomes we consistently see that more positive outcomes, such as higher worker commitment, motivation and performance – as judged by the managers – are associated with use and wide application of more human resource practices, effective use of job-related communication devices and keeping more of the promises made. It should be noted that the keeping of promises is itself affected by the number of human resource practices in place and the effectiveness of job-related and induction-related communication. Using the psychological contract in employment relations has a small but consistently positive additional association with outcomes. Of course, we need to be careful in a cross-sectional survey about making any claims about causality. We can report a number of associations that fit with the model and imply a causal direction from policy and practice to outcomes. There is sufficient evidence elsewhere, including the CIPD survey on change and the psychological contract (Guest and Conway 2001), to indicate support for the causal model. The various key links that emerged from the study are summarised in Figure 22.

While job-related communication has a consistently positive association with outcomes, the other two sets of communication practices have a more variable link. Induction-related communication has no association with any of the

specific outcomes, although it is linked to the overall assessment of the impact of keeping promises and commitments. This is not surprising since it is likely to have its impact at the outset of employment with the organisation rather than on a day-to-day basis. Top-down communication has a positive association with some outcomes, but most notably with commitment of workers to the organisation and the commitment of the organisation to its workers. The lack of significant associations is not a case for neglecting communication of the psychological contract at

Figure 22 | A summary of the main findings from the survey

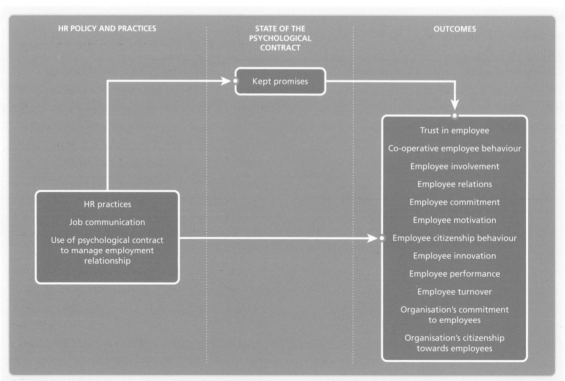

Note

The state of the psychological contract, the number of widely applied human resource practices and the use of the psychological contract to manage the employment relationship were related to all 12 outcomes; job communication, however, was related to 11 out of the 12 outcomes.

> 'In evaluating the state of the psychological contract and the employment relationship, managers are cautiously positive.'

the outset of employment. At the same time the results confirm the greater impact of the regular and local communication over more selective and more occasional approaches.

Organisational factors explaining variations in the psychological contract

Turning to other background factors, the results show that size of organisation tends to have a negative association with outcomes. Managers appear most certain that larger organisations are poorer at meeting their obligations to their employees rather than vice versa. Managers also persistently rate outcomes lower where there is a recognised trade union. The exceptions to this are involvement, where one of the questions implied a representative role, and labour retention, with which unions have long been associated. It is unclear from this analysis why a union presence should result in lower trust, co-operation, motivation, performance and so on. However, it does suggest that managers find it more difficult to manage the employment relationship where a trade union is present and less easy to win the hearts and minds of workers.

There is some evidence of more positive outcomes in the public than in the private sector. Public sector workers are reported to be more committed, motivated, involved and innovative. Their job performance is also rated more highly. This is something of a surprise because managers in the public sector are most likely to report that promises are not kept. Herein lies the probable explanation. The statistical analysis controlled for the extent to which promises were kept. What we therefore see is evidence that in those parts of the public sector where promises are kept, then the outcomes tend to be more positive than where

they are kept in the private sector. Overall, then, because promises are less often kept in the public sector, the public sector results are no better and, if anything, slightly worse than the private sector. This is reflected in the correlations in the appendices. What it implies is that there is the potential for high commitment, motivation and performance in the public sector if only management could keep its promises. As we have noted earlier in the report, the CIPD survey of the psychological contract among workers in the public sector (Guest and Conway 2000) revealed similar findings. Among central government workers in particular, there was a strong feeling that management failed to keep its promises. Apparently the personnel managers in the sector agree with this view.

A positive psychological contract?

In evaluating the state of the psychological contract and the employment relationship, managers are cautiously positive. They are cautious first in terms of their willingness to state positively that they make firm promises and commitments across a range of issues. Second, they are cautiously positive about both the effectiveness of their communication practices and their ability to keep promises. Finally, they generally believe that employees' attitudes and behaviour are positive. The caution is reflected in a reluctance to offer extreme responses; the managers are more comfortable 'agreeing' than 'strongly agreeing' about issues. As already noted, this may genuinely reflect a moderately positive outcome or a degree of uncertainty about making general statements when there is either variety of response among the workforce or a degree of ignorance about some of the outcomes. It is certainly possible that some of these senior managers are not in a good position

'Delivery of promises and commitments is a key issue for collaboration between personnel and line managers.'

to know the outcomes on the ground in anything other than general terms. Once again, this is why case studies are needed to complement these findings and get under-the-surface responses.

While the assessment of managers is generally positive across the range of attitudes and behaviours, there are two outcomes where the picture is rather different. The first concerns employee involvement. Approximately 40 per cent agreed and 40 per cent disagreed that employees and their representatives were involved in organisation-wide decisions, but only 24 per cent agreed while 52 per cent disagreed that employees were involved in decisions made by the organisation affecting jobs. There has been much discussion about employee involvement and partnership, but it appears from this evidence that in many organisations employees and their representatives are excluded from decisions that can have a direct bearing upon their employment. This is one of the few outcomes where a union presence is associated with a more positive response, if we assume that greater employee involvement is positive. The second outcome concerns innovation. Only 31 per cent agreed that there is a great deal of innovation coming from employees and 24 per cent expressed satisfaction with the level of innovation and new ideas from employees, compared with 43 per cent who were dissatisfied. We know from other studies that innovation is likely to be greater where managers request, encourage and reward innovation. It would appear from these results that despite the generally positive view of employee performance, there is scope to focus attention more strongly on some key aspects such as involvement and innovative behaviour.

There is some indication that in the contemporary employment relationship the balance of power has shifted towards management; some might say too far towards management. When we asked managers about the commitment of workers and their role as good citizens, willing to put themselves out for the organisation, managers generally gave a positive response. When we asked them the same questions about the organisation, the level of positive response was similar or slightly lower. By implication the balance of commitment and contribution is leaning towards workers. They contribute as much if not more to the organisation than they get in return. We might expect this assessment from workers, but when it comes from senior managers with some responsibility for employment relations policy and practice then we should take it very seriously.

Policy implications

Finally, we can list some of the policy implications emerging from this report. The first is that the psychological contract appears to offer a viable framework within which to consider aspects of contemporary employment relations and to formulate relevant policy. There is clearly scope for considerable further development of the framework outlined in this report. The results confirm the findings from separate surveys of employees showing that where the organisation provides more input to the employment relationship, reflected largely in its extensive use of a range of progressive, high commitment human resource practices, and delivers on its promises and commitments, then workers will respond positively and this will be reflected in their attitudes and behaviour. Indeed, the use of human resource practices generally implies promises, and senior managers need to be aware of this when they promulgate certain promises and need to ensure that they provide the other resources necessary to ensure that implementation is possible. In this context, it is interesting that a number of managers highlighted health and safety and the working environment as areas where promises had been made but not kept.

The two core policy recommendations are therefore:

◻ It makes sense to introduce and effectively implement a range of progressive human resource practices of the sort listed in Chapter 3 of this report.

◻ Organisations should not make promises they cannot keep.

Delivery of promises and commitments is a key issue for collaboration between personnel and line managers. This appears to have been a particular problem in the public sector, but it is a risk wherever centralised policies and practices are developed and communicated without the resources to implement them. It is also a warning against sudden enthusiasms for fads and fashions that burst upon organisations but are soon left neglected. These simple recommendations are hardly rocket science; rather, they are a further plea for good management. But they are offered in the context of yet another survey showing the low level of adoption of the kind of practices that are most likely to lead to an effective employment relationship and positive outcomes for both organisation and workers.

References

CULLY M., WOODLAND S., O'REILLY A. and DIX G. (1999)

Britain at Work – as depicted by the 1998 Workplace Employee Relations Survey. London, Routledge.

GUEST D. and CONWAY N. (2000)

The Psychological Contract in the Public Sector. London, CIPD.

GUEST D. and CONWAY N. (2001)

Organisational Change and the Psychological Contract. London, CIPD.

GUEST D., MICHIE J., SHEEHAN M., CONWAY N. and METOCHI M. (2000)

Effective People Management: Initial findings of the Future of Work study. London, CIPD.

HERRIOT P. and PEMBERTON C. (1995)

New Deals: The revolution in managerial careers. Chichester, Wiley.

KOTTER J. P. (1973)

'The psychological contract: managing the joining up process'. *California Management Review.* Vol. 15, Nos. 91–99.

MILLWARD N., BRYSON A. and FORTH J. (2000)

All Change at Work? London, Routledge.

ROUSSEAU D. (1995)

Psychological Contracts in Organizations. Thousand Oaks, Calif., Sage.

Appendix 1

Descriptive summary of sample

Background variable	Category	Percentage of sample
Company size	Fewer than 10 employees	1.4
	10–24 employees	2.7
	25–99 employees	6.6
	100–499 employees	19.6
	500–999 employees	11.0
	1,000–4,999 employees	28.0
	5,000–9,999 employees	10.8
	10,000–19,999 employees	7.1
	Over 20,000 employees	12.9
Establishment size	Fewer than 10 employees	3.9
	10–24 employees	6.0
	25–99 employees	17.9
	100–499 employees	39.7
	500–999 employees	12.6
	1,000 or more employees	19.8
Sector	Private (manufacturing)	20.4
	Private (services)	42.6
	Private (utilities)	2.7
	Public sector	34.2
Trade union recognition	No	38.9
	Yes	61.1
Proportion of employees belonging to the trade union	Less than 25%	19.8
	25–50%	29.5
	51–75%	33.6
	Over 75%	17.1
Department the respondent primarily worked in	Personnel/HR/Training	86.0
	Other	14.0
Job level of respondent	Director	21.6
	Senior executive/group role	40.1
	Manager	33.3
	Senior officer	5.0
Tenure	Up to 5 years	43.8
	5–10 years	23.3
	10–15 years	13.0
	More than 15 years	19.9

Appendix 2

Measurement of variables

The table below describes how variables used in the path analysis were constructed from items included in the questionnaire. For the antecedents, the psychological contract and outcomes, the item wordings and percentage responses are reported in the main body of the text. Alpha reliability coefficients for multiple item measures are presented in Appendix 3.

Variable name	Description
BACKGROUND FACTORS	
Company size	Single item, ranging from 1 = fewer than 10 employees to 10 = over 20,000 employees.
Establishment size	Single item, ranging from 1 = fewer than 10 employees to 6 = 1,000 or more employees.
Public sector	Single item where respondents were asked whether their organisation belonged to the public sector (coded 1) or private sector (coded 0).
Trade union presence	Single item, where respondent was asked whether their organisation had a recognised trade union or a recognised staff association (coded 1) or not (coded 0).
Department respondent works in	Single item, where respondent was asked which department he or she primarily worked in. The HR department was coded 1; other departments were coded 0.
Job level of respondent	Single item, where respondents indicated their job level. Directors and senior executives were coded 1; managers and senior officers were coded 0.
Tenure	Single item, where respondents indicated how long they had worked for the organisation.
ANTECEDENTS	
HR practices	This variable is a count across 14 items assessing HR practices. For each item, if the practice applied to more than half the workforce, one was added to the count, else zero.
Organisational communication	Respondents were presented with a list of 13 items assessing the effectiveness of methods used by the organisation to communicate its promises and commitments to employees. The rating scale ranged from 'not at all effective' to 'very effective', with a further response separated from the scale of 'not used'. The usage of methods of communication was a count across the 13 items, with used coded as 1 and not used coded as 0. A factor analysis of the effectiveness of methods of communications revealed three factors consisting of job communication (6 items), initial and bureaucratic communication (4 items) and corporate downward communication (2 items). One of the items loads heavily on two factors ('Other briefing groups') and was removed from the factor analysis.
THE PSYCHOLOGICAL CONTRACT	
Promises made	Thirteen items, where respondents reported the extent to which the organisation had promised or committed itself to provide a list of items typically used in psychological contract research.
Promises kept	Where promises had been explicitly made or strongly suggested, respondents were asked to indicate the extent promises had been kept.
OUTCOMES	
Employees' attitudes, employee behaviours and organisational outcomes	Twelve measures, each consisting of two items, were used including: employee commitment, performance, motivation, innovation, citizenship behaviour, co-operation and turnover; and the organisation's trust, commitment, citizenship and relations with employees.

Notes on statistical procedures

1 Reliability of variables

Cronbach's Alpha coefficient was used to assess the reliability of multiple item constructs in the analysis. It is generally considered that Cronbach's Alpha represents good internal consistency when the coefficient is above 0.8, acceptable in the 0.7 range and poor when less than 0.6.

2 Path analysis

The figures in the report are a summary of standard multiple regressions using SPSS for Windows, Version 8. The numbers displayed in boxes lying on the lines running from left to right represent the standardised (beta) coefficients from the regression analysis. A 'significant' beta weight ('*') has an associated p-value less than 0.05, a 'strongly significant' beta weight ('**') has an associated p-value less than 0.01, and a 'very strongly significant' beta weight ('***') has an associated p-value less than 0.001. The boxes with arrows going into them are the dependent variables in the regression run.

The labels beneath the dependent variables ('Adj Rsq') stand for the adjusted R-square. The adjusted R-square provides a more conservative estimate of the amount of variance that is explained in the dependent variable by the independent variables. The number of independent variables associated with the regression equation inflates the magnitude of the unadjusted R-square; hence the adjusted R-square corrects for this by taking into account the number of independent variables.

Appendix 3

Correlations between variables used in the study[1, 2]

	1	2	3	4	5	6	7	8	9	10	11	12	13	14	15	16	17	18	19	20	21	22	23	24	25
1. Organisation size																									
2. Establishment size	.61																								
3. Public sector	.13	.15																							
4. Union	.45	.33	.46																						
5. HR dept[3]	.13	.18	−.07	.04																					
6. Senior manager[4]	−.21	−.14	−.06	−.11	−.04																				
7. Use PC[5]	−.03	−.01	−.06	−.04	.00	.05																			
8. HR practices	.08	.13	.00	.08	−.04	.07	.26	(.77)																	
9. Job communication	−.10	−.08	−.10	−.06	−.02	.14	.19	.52	(.82)																
10. Top-down communication	−.08	−.05	−.13	−.10	−.06	.11	.17	.40	.46	(.69)															
11. Initial communication[6]	−.11	−.06	−.04	−.08	.02	.09	.12	.31	.45	.38	(.67)														
12. Promises made	.08	.09	−.07	.00	−.04	.08	.21	.56	.43	.38	.31	(.81)													
13. Promises kept	−.19	−.10	−.21	−.15	−.03	.17	.16	.35	.43	.31	.38	.28	(.86)												
14. Employee performance	−.10	−.03	.00	−.10	−.05	.09	.16	.32	.35	.21	.22	.28	.32	(.77)											
15. Employee motivation	−.11	−.04	−.05	−.15	−.06	.17	.21	.36	.39	.26	.21	.33	.36	.63	(.82)										
16. Employee relations	−.16	−.10	−.16	−.15	−.05	.21	.27	.40	.45	.35	.31	.36	.46	.49	.63	(.75)									
17. Trust in employees	−.12	−.05	−.08	−.13	−.10	.07	.17	.28	.29	.22	.19	.24	.34	.54	.53	.56	(.63)								
18. Organisation's comm't	−.19	−.09	−.03	−.12	−.03	.26	.23	.40	.41	.36	.31	.38	.44	.32	.48	.62	.36	(.83)							
19. Employee innovation	−.09	−.04	−.01	−.09	−.07	.01	.17	.30	.28	.24	.15	.27	.28	.48	.45	.34	.34	.27	(.74)						
20. Organisation's OCBs	−.18	−.07	−.09	−.12	−.02	.23	.26	.43	.42	.35	.31	.40	.46	.32	.44	.56	.32	.74	.36	(.74)					
21. Employee turnover	.11	.04	.02	−.03	.05	−.17	−.14	−.31	−.27	−.19	−.18	−.23	−.35	−.26	−.35	−.39	−.29	−.37	−.20	−.36	(.59)				
22. Employee OCBs	−.09	−.08	−.11	−.16	−.09	.11	.15	.27	.30	.22	.15	.25	.28	.54	.57	.53	.59	.32	.41	.33	−.30	(.71)			
23. Employee co-operation	−.12	−.07	−.15	−.20	−.08	.14	.16	.30	.34	.27	.22	.25	.33	.54	.53	.60	.58	.34	.37	.36	−.31	.66	(.66)		
24. Employee involvement	−.09	−.03	.19	.13	−.09	.12	.25	.47	.38	.33	.25	.33	.30	.24	.33	.44	.29	.49	.31	.46	−.31	.22	.27	(.74)	
25. Employee commitment	−.12	−.07	−.03	−.13	−.06	.15	.27	.38	.37	.38	.25	.32	.36	.49	.67	.63	.54	.55	.40	.47	−.38	.55	.51	.41	(.68)

Notes

1 Correlations greater than 0.06 are significant at the 0.05 level (2-tailed); greater than 0.08 are significant at the 0.01 level; greater than 0.10 are significant at the 0.001 level.

2 Figures in brackets along the diagonal represent Alpha reliability coefficients for multiple item measures.

3 Respondent works in an HR department.

4 Respondent is in a senior management position.

5 The psychological contract is explicitly used by the organisation to manage employee relations.

6 The three measures of communication refer to communication effectiveness.